W9-BDI-283

Reading Mastery
Signature Edition

Textbook C

Siegfried Engelmann
Susan Hanner

SRA

A Division of The McGraw-Hill Companies
Columbus, Ohio

Illustration Credits

Dave Blanchette, Mark Corcoran, Susan DeMarco, John
Edwards and Associates, Karen Pritchett, Simon Galkin,
Meryl Henderson, Susan Jerde, Loretta Lustig, Lauren
Simeone, and James Shough.

Reading Mastery® is a registered trademark of the McGraw-Hill Companies, Inc.

SRAonline.com

 SRA

A Division of The McGraw-Hill Companies

Copyright © 2008 by SRA/McGraw-Hill.

All rights reserved. No part of this publication may be
reproduced or distributed in any form or by any means,
or stored in a database or retrieval system, without the
prior written consent of The McGraw-Hill Companies,
Inc., including, but not limited to, network storage or
transmission, or broadcast for distance learning.

Printed in the United States of America.

Send all inquiries to this address:
SRA/McGraw-Hill
4400 Easton Commons
Columbus, OH 43219

ISBN: 978-0-07-612543-2
MHID: 0-07-612543-2

16 17 18 19 20 QVS 20 19 18 17 16

Table of Contents

Lesson   **page**   **Lesson**   **page**

101 Andrew Begins to
Change 1

102 Andrew Plays Harder .. 8

103 The Titans Play
Harder 16

104 Andrew Leaves the
Team 23

105 The Championship
Game.............. 30

106 The End of the Game 37

107 Places You Have Learned
About. 45
Looking for
Treasures........... 48

108 Words That Talk 56
Hohoboho 57

109 Liz Takes a Trip...... 62
The Words That Sat
in the Back Rows..... 64

110 Test 11............. 70

111 Facts About Canada .. 73
The Big Change in
Hohoboho 74

112 Run Gets Moved 81

113 Facts About Australia . 88
Toby the Kangaroo... 90

114 Facts About
Kangaroos.......... 97
A Job for Toby 98

115 Facts About
Peacocks 105
The Kangaroo
Hunters 106

116 Facts About Minutes.. 112
Facts About Ships ... 113
Toby on the Ship.... 113

117 The End of the Trip.. 120

118 More Facts About
Canada 126
The Ship Arrives in
Canada 127

119 Facts About a
Circus............ 133
Toby's New Job..... 135

120 Test 12............ 141

121 Facts About Boxing .. 145
Toby Leaves the
Circus............ 146

122 The Big Fight 152
Special Project 159

123 Homonyms......... 160
The Scarred Words in the
Word Bank........ 161

124 Henry Ouch Takes a
Vacation.......... 166
The Number with the
Most Scars........ 167

125 A Pilot's Trip....... 172
Some Words Stop
Fighting 173

126 Another Change Is
Made 178

127 Contractions........ 184
The Last Problem in the
Word Bank Is Solved.. 185

128 Wooden Buildings ... 190

Lesson		page
	Time Machines	191
	More About a Time Line	192
129	Eric and Tom Find a Time Machine	199
130	Test 13	207
131	More About Time	210
	The San Francisco Earthquake	211
132	More About Time	220
	Facts About Egypt	221
	Eric and Tom in Egypt	222
133	More About Time	228
	Eric and Tom Go to a Palace	229
134	Inventing	238
	Eric and Tom Meet the King	239
135	Eric and Tom Leave Egypt	244
136	A Queen Named Helen	251
	Eric and Tom in Greece	252
137	Forty Thousand Years Ago	258
	Eric and Tom See Cave People	259

Lesson		page
138	More About Time	266
	Eric and Tom in the City of the Future	267
139	More About Time	274
	North America	275
	Spain in 1492	276
140	Test 14	283
141	More About Time	288
	The Dog and the Time Machine	289
142	Vikings	296
	The Land of the Vikings	297
143	More About Time	304
	Trying to Get Home	306
144	Facts About the United States	313
	Concord	314
145	More About Time	322
	Home	324
	End-of-Program Test	331
	Special Project	336
	Fact Game Answer Key	337
	Vocabulary Sentences	340
	Glossary	343
	Index	360

A

1

1. <u>re</u>porters
2. <u>them</u>selves
3. <u>mem</u>bers
4. <u>prac</u>tices
5. <u>chan</u>ces

2

1. noticed
2. realized
3. dressed
4. squeezed
5. frightened

3

1. packed
2. still
3. comment
4. awful
5. commented

4

1. Handy Andy
2. firing
3. towel
4. newspapers
5. holler

B

Andrew Begins to Change

The newspapers were filled with stories about Andrew. They called him "Handy Andy, the man who does it all for the Titans." Andrew was very busy. He had to go to the practices. He also had to talk to reporters. And when he left the practice field every day, a group of fans would be outside. They wanted him to sign his name in their books.

Andrew didn't daydream anymore. His life was like a great daydream so he didn't have time for anything except living. He worked very hard. And the other members of the Titans started to work hard, too. They started to become proud of themselves and proud of their team.

Before Andrew had come around, people would say to the other players, "Oh, you play for that awful team, the Titans." Now the people would say, "Wow, you play with the Titans. They are the hottest team in football." The players wanted to show the fans that the team wasn't just a one-man team. They wanted to show that there were 11 good football players on the field when the Titans played.

When the players played better, the coaches didn't yell as much. Before Andrew came along, you would never hear Denny say, "Good job." But now, he would frequently holler to his players, "That's the way to run that play. Good job."

And the people who owned the Titans didn't tell Denny they were thinking of firing him. Instead, they asked things like this: "What do you think our chances are for winning the championship?"

Denny would reply, "Our chances of winning the championship are pretty good if we keep playing the way we're playing."

And the fans were happy. The people who lived in Andrew's city felt that the team was their team. They talked about the team. People who didn't know each other would talk on the bus or in the grocery store. "Did you see Handy Andy and the Titans last Sunday?" they would say. Then they would start talking about the game.

Every Sunday the stands were packed. There were no empty seats. And when the Titans came onto the field, the fans would cheer. The fans would think, "That's my team and it's the best team there is. Yea for the Titans."

For five Sundays, it was the same. Andrew would come onto the ⭐ field when the team couldn't move. He would either kick the ball or run with it. When he kicked, he would usually make a field goal. When he ran with it he would always make a touchdown. Nobody could stop him. Sometimes three or four players would hit him at the same time. For those players, running into Andrew was just like running into the side of a truck. They bounced back and Andrew kept going.

But then on the sixth Sunday, Andrew felt strange. When he was getting dressed for the game, he noticed that his hands and feet were tingling. He had the same feeling that he had felt earlier at Magnetic Research Company when he had walked into the room filled with electricity.

Now he was sitting on the bench in front of his locker putting his shoes on. Suddenly, he realized what was wrong. He grabbed the locker handle and squeezed it as hard as he could. Instead of bending it like a piece of clay, he put a tiny dent in it. He tried again. The outcome was the same. Andrew Dexter was losing his super strength.

He was still strong, perhaps as strong as a quarter horse, which meant that he was probably as strong as five or six very strong men. But he didn't have the strength of an African elephant anymore.

He was frightened. If he was getting weaker and weaker, he would soon lose all his super strength. He would just be plain old Andrew Dexter again. Mean George walked by the bench and slapped Andrew on the back. "Big game today," Mean George said. "You're going to do it for us again today."

"George," Andrew said, looking up at the huge man. "I . . . I don't think I'm going to be . . . I don't . . . "

"What's the matter, man?" George said and sat next to Andrew. The bench bent down under the weight of Mean George. "Andy, you look sick."

Andrew said, "You guys are going to have to help me out. I don't think I'll be able to run or kick as well today."

"You've got to," George said. "Without you, we're just a bunch of bums."

"No," Andrew shouted. "Don't you say that. You guys are great. You just don't know it. You can do it without me. You just have to tell yourselves that you can."

MORE NEXT TIME

C **Number your paper from 1 through 15.**

Review Items

1. When we talk about how hot or cold something is, we tell about the ▮▮▮▮ of the thing.

2. How fast does a jumbo jet fly?
   - 5 miles per hour   • 50 miles per hour
   - 500 miles per hour

3. Write the name of the city that's on the east coast.

4. Write the name of the city that's on the west coast.

5. Which letter shows where Denver is?

6. Which letter shows where Chicago is?

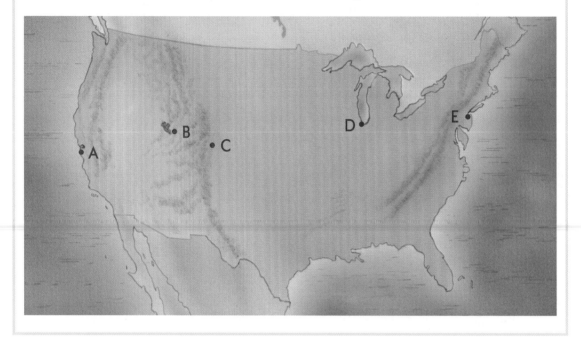

7. Let's say you are outside when the temperature is 40 degrees. What is the temperature inside your body?

8. Let's say a fly is outside when the temperature is 40 degrees. What is the temperature inside the fly's body?

9. Let's say you are outside when the temperature is 85 degrees. What is the temperature inside your body?

10. Write the letter of the animal that is facing into the wind.

11. Which direction is that animal facing?

12. So what's the **name** of that wind?

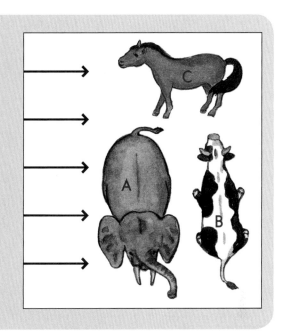

13. What is the temperature of the water in each jar?

14. Write the letter of each jar that is filled with ocean water.

15. Jar B is not filled with ocean water. How do you know?

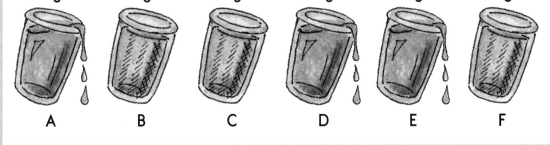

32 degrees   32 degrees   32 degrees   32 degrees   32 degrees   32 degrees

A   B   C   D   E   F

A

1
1. hinge
2. unusual
3. block
4. showers
5. towel

2
1. count on
2. mean
3. wild
4. wildly
5. experts

3
1. comment
2. mates
3. teammates
4. commenting

B

Andrew Plays Harder

Andrew didn't mean to shout at Mean George. But Andrew was frightened. Andrew didn't want to go back to being plain old Andrew Dexter. He wanted to keep on being Handy Andy. Mean George said, "Hey man, you can count on me. I'll give the Titans everything I got. But we want you out there with us. We need you."

"I'll do the best I can," Andrew said.

When Andrew had been as strong as an elephant, he hadn't tried to play as hard as he could have. He didn't want to hurt the other players. So he ran just hard enough to get past the other players.

Now that Andrew's strength was fading, he tried harder. In the next game that Andrew played, he kicked the ball with all his strength. When his first kick was sailing through the air, the announcer said, "That's not much of a kick for Handy Andy, but it's still something to watch. It must have a hang-time of over six seconds. Not bad."

During that game, Andrew was tackled for the first time. He tried to run through the other team instead of kicking the ball. Three players hit him at the same time. Andrew tried to keep his feet under him, but the players brought him down to the ground.

Andrew was tackled three other times during that game. He was tackled four times, but he also scored four touchdowns. When Andrew got tackled, the other players on the Titans didn't yell at him. They said, "Good try, man. We'll do a better job of blocking for you."

"Thanks," Andrew said.

The game was close, but the Titans won it. The fans cheered for Andrew. They held up signs that said things like HANDY ANDY IS A DANDY, and WITH ANDY THE TITANS ARE NUMBER ONE. But when the game was over, Andrew Dexter

sat on the bench in the locker room. He could hardly catch his breath. His hands were tingling. So were his legs and feet. His body was losing power by the second.

He wiped his sweaty face with a towel. His mind was racing. What would he do now? How long would it be before he lost all his strength? How could the Titans win the championship if he lost his strength? What  would the fans do when he went out on the field and couldn't kick the ball any farther than any bank teller could? What would they say when he couldn't run any faster than any other man could run?

The fans would boo. They would throw things onto the field. Andrew could see them in his mind. "Boo," they would yell. "Get that bum off the field." Andrew could almost hear them. He buried his head in the towel. He felt like crying.

"Good game, man."

Andrew didn't look up. He felt the bench bend down as somebody sat next to him. "We're going to do a better job next week," the voice said. It was Mean George. "We didn't do a good job of blocking for you today. But next week, not one of those guys is going to get near you. You'll run down the field like you're all alone."

Andrew wiped his eyes and looked up. "Thanks, George," he said. "But I don't think I'll be able to play next week. I . . . " He shook his head and then buried it in the towel again. Andrew didn't want George to see the tears in his eyes.

"What's this talk about not playing?" George asked, and slapped Andrew on the back. "Of course you're going to play. You're part of this team, right?"

"Yeah," Andrew said, looking up.

"Then you play on this team. I play and you play."

Andrew smiled. "I'll do my best," Andrew said.

"So will we," Mean George said.

• • •

There is a difference between players when they play to win and the same players when they are just playing. You could see that difference during the practices all week long. The Titans ran their plays with a little more power, a little more speed, and with all the players trying harder—a lot harder.

Andrew watched the team and he was proud of them. They weren't blaming each other or blaming the coaches. They weren't arguing. They were trying hard and practicing as if they were champions.

But Andrew didn't feel like a champion. His strength was no longer that of a quarter horse. It had faded to the strength of a Mongolian horse. Of course he was still much stronger than even the strongest man; however, his strength was fading.

MORE NEXT TIME

C Number your paper from 1 through 17.

Review Items

1. Which letter shows where San Francisco is?
2. If you were in San Francisco, which direction would you face if you wanted the wind to blow in your face?

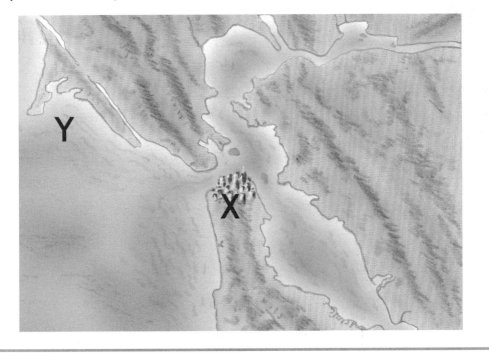

3. The United States is a ▬▬▬.   • city • state • country
4. Japan is a ▬▬▬.
5. How many states are in the United States?

6. Would it be easier to catch a fly on **a hot day** or **a cold day?**
7. Tell why.

8. Which letter shows where Italy is?

9. Which letter shows where China is?

10. Which letter shows where Turkey is?

11. Which letter shows where Japan is?

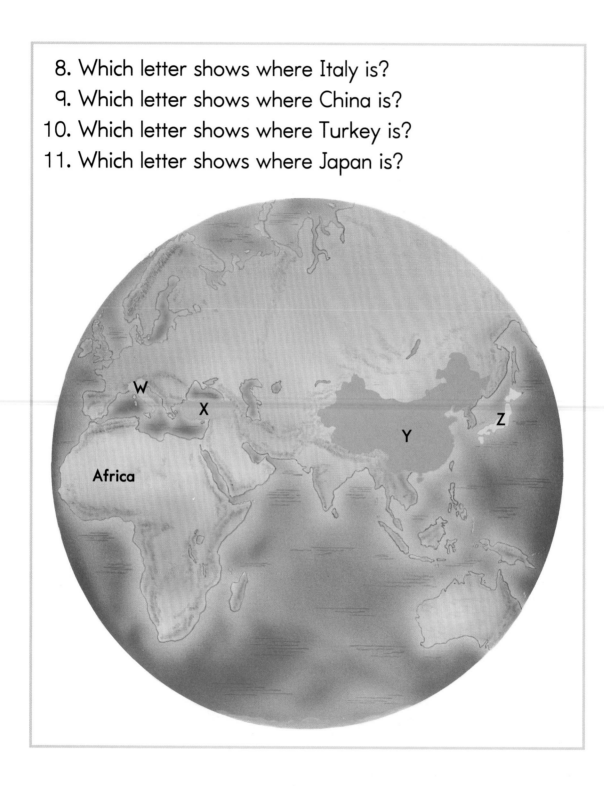

12. All machines make it easier for someone to ▮▮▮.

13. The arrow that killed Achilles hit him in the ▮▮▮.

14. That arrow had something on it that killed Achilles. What did it have on it?

Here's how fast different things can go:
- 20 miles per hour
- 35 miles per hour
- 200 miles per hour
- 500 miles per hour

15. Which speed tells how fast a fast man can run?

16. Which speed tells how fast a jet can fly?

17. Which speed tells how fast a fast dog can run?

A

1
1. breakfast
2. television
3. receive
4. ache

2
1. hinge
2. wildly
3. teammates
4. unusual

B The Titans Play Harder

The Titans practiced hard all week. Andrew kicked the ball four times during the game on Sunday. But not one of his hang-times was six seconds. The shortest hang-time was just under five seconds, and the longest hang-time was just under six seconds. Andrew carried the ball ten times during that game. He scored one touchdown. He tried to make his legs move as fast as they could. And that was very fast. He still had the strength of a small horse. With all that power in his legs, he could run faster than any man alive. He hadn't tried to use all his speed before, but he knew that he could be tackled. He ran as hard as he could so he could stay away from the players on the other team.

The Titans were one point behind with less than a minute to go. The Titans had the ball. They were fifty yards from the goal line. They decided to try a field goal, with Andrew kicking the ball. The crowd was cheering wildly. If he made this field goal, the Titans would win and they would be in the championship game for the Professional Football League. If he missed, the Titans would lose the game and would not be in the championship game.

Andrew's heart was pounding. He kept reminding himself to think about kicking the ball and to think of nothing else. "Watch the ball. Keep your head down. Take two steps. Kick it just under the middle of the ball. Watch the ball. Keep your head down . . . "

The ball was put in place. Andrew took two quick steps forward. He kept his head down. He kicked it, just below the middle of the ball. For a moment he didn't look up. In the distance, he heard the sound of players' shoulder pads hitting other shoulder pads. He heard the whooping sound of the crowd—then a second of almost silence. And then he heard wild cheers. Just as Andrew looked up, the ball sailed between the upright poles. The kick was good. The Titans had scored three more points and had won the game. In two weeks, they would be in the championship game.

The locker room was wild. Reporters and TV cameras were everywhere. There were lights and owners and coaches and players and a lot of shouting: "We're number one!"

"Tell me," a voice said. There were lights in Andrew's eyes. On the other side of the lights was the outline of a

TV camera. "Tell me how it feels to be in the championship game."

"I feel great," Andrew said. "We have a great team, and we're going to win the championship."

"You'll be playing the Wildcats. Many experts think that they are the strongest team in the league."

Andrew said, "They're a good team, but we beat them once this year already. We're going to try to beat them again."

"That was a great game you played today" the announcer said. "A lot of people were commenting on your speed. We had never seen you run that fast before. In fact, we didn't know you had so much speed."

Andrew didn't know what to say. "I had a lot of help today. My teammates did a great job of blocking for me."

The yelling and smiling and cheering went on for nearly an hour. Then the players took showers, got dressed, and left. The last player in the locker room was Andrew. He sat in front of his locker and said goodbye to each player. Then, when the locker room was empty, Andrew grabbed the handle of his locker and squeezed it as hard as he could. He couldn't make a dent in the steel handle.

"Two weeks," Andrew said to himself, and he felt frightened. "If only I could keep my strength for two weeks." Of course, Andrew wanted to be a star and wanted to have people love him and think he was great. But as he sat there in that still locker room, with only the sound of dripping showers, he wanted the championship for his teammates.

Andrew imagined how the Titans would look if they could win the championship. He imagined how they would feel. They would feel proud. And Andrew wanted them to feel proud. But he was beginning to think that he wouldn't be able to help them. His hands and feet were tingling. In only three weeks, his strength had faded from that of an elephant to that of a small horse. What would happen in two more weeks?

MORE NEXT TIME

C Number your paper from 1 through 17.

Skill Items

> **She commented about the still water.**
> 1. What word means **silent** or **peaceful**?
> 2. What word means quickly **told** about something?

Review Items

Write **W** for warm-blooded animals and **C** for cold-blooded animals.

3. beetle

4. spider

5. horse

6. cow

7. bee

8. When a plane flies from New York City to San Francisco, is it flying in the **same direction** or the **opposite direction** as the wind?

9. How far is it from New York City to San Francisco?

10. How far is it from San Francisco to Japan?

11. What ocean do you cross to get from San Francisco to Japan?

12. Write the letter of each place that is in the United States.
   a. Alaska   f. Turkey   j. California
   b. Italy   g. China   k. Ohio
   c. New York City   h. Japan   l. San Francisco
   d. Lake Michigan   i. Chicago   m. Texas
   e. Denver

13. Write the letters of the 5 names that tell about length.
      a. minute   g. mile
      b. meter   h. yard
      c. day   i. year
      d. centimeter   j. inch
      e. second   k. hour
      f. week

14. A mile is a little more than ▮▮▮ feet.
   • 1 thousand   • 5 thousand   • 5 hundred

15. You can see drops of water on grass early in the morning. What are those drops called?

16. You would have the most power if you pushed against one of the handles. Which handle is that?

17. Which handle would give you the least amount of power?

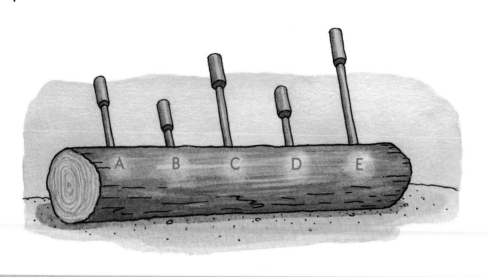

A

1	2	3
1. squeals	1. shame	1. let somebody down
2. received	2. shamed	2. harm
3. ached	3. ashamed	3. rise
4. hinges	4. honest	4. signal
5. signaled	5. television	5. grocery
	6. breakfast	6. unusual

B # Andrew Leaves the Team

❀ Andrew's super strength had faded completely. It was now a week before the championship. "Denny," he told the coach, "I can't play in the championship game."

Denny was standing on the sideline with a whistle in his mouth when Andrew made this announcement. Denny almost swallowed the whistle. Denny coughed and stared at Andrew with big eyes. "You can't <u>what</u>?"

"I can't play," Andrew explained. "I couldn't do the team any good."

"Of course you can do us good. We need you. I mean, you've been the star of this team ever since you came to us. What's . . . "

Andrew shook his head. "I lost my strength," Andrew said. "I can't kick and I can't run. I won't do you any good."

"Maybe you need to rest for a couple of days," Denny said. "Why don't you take it easy for a few days. We've got time. Your strength will come back. You'll be just as good as you ever were."

"No, Coach," Andrew said. "I'm through. I can't play." Andrew shook his head. He tried to say, "I want to thank you for letting me play with the Titans," but his voice wouldn't work. His voice came out like a little squeak. He shook his head, looked down, took a deep breath, and said, "Good luck." Then he ran off the field to the locker room.

Within a couple of minutes, most of the players were crowding around Andrew. "You can't leave us now," Mean George said. "You are a part of this team. We play, you play."

"I'd like to play," Andrew said, looking down. "But if I'm out there, I won't help you. I'll hurt you. I've got no strength. I'm . . . "

"Are you hurt?" one of the players asked.

"I can't explain," Andrew said. "But honest, I've got no more strength."

"Hey," George said to the other players. "Let Andy alone. Just get out of here. He'll be all right."

The other players left the locker room. Mean George slapped Andrew Dexter on the back. It hurt. "You just take it easy, Andy," he said. "Everything is going to be all right."

Outside the park four teenagers were waiting for Andrew. He ✦ signed their books. One of them said, "The Titans are going to kill the Wildcats next Sunday, right Andy?"

"They're going to play as hard as they can," Andrew said.

But when Sunday came around, Andrew decided not to go to the ball park. He felt ashamed. He didn't want to let the Titans down, but he knew that he couldn't help them. He had planned to watch the game on TV. He felt sick. He hadn't slept well the night before. He imagined the faces of the players and the coaches when he didn't show up. He imagined how they would feel after coming so close to winning the championship. Andrew wanted to see them cheer and shout and hold up their fists as they yelled, "We're number one." But in his mind he could see them walking to the locker room after the game with their heads down. He saw the tears on their faces. He saw the sadness in the faces of the crowd.

Andrew ate breakfast. The phone rang three times but he didn't answer it. The doorbell rang and rang, but he didn't answer the door. He sat there trying to eat his eggs and toast. He wasn't hungry, and eating the toast was like eating paper. He couldn't seem to swallow. At last he gave up and turned on his old television set. Nothing happened. He examined the set, but everything seemed to be all right. Then he thought that the wall plug might not be in right. He wiggled the plug from side to side. The electric cord that went from the plug to the television set was worn out.

When Andrew moved the plug from side to side, his finger touched the bare metal inside the electric cord. When his finger touched the bare metal, Andrew received a terrible electric shock. It knocked him over and almost knocked him out. His teeth ached because he had bitten down so hard from the shock. His arm felt as if somebody had hit it with a hammer. And his fingers tingled. And his feet tingled. And his legs tingled.

MORE NEXT TIME

C Number your paper from 1 through 18.

Skill Items

Use the words in the box to write complete sentences.

| received | argued | still | realized | commented |
| championship | unusual | frequently | chances |

1. He ▮▮▮▮ ▮▮▮▮ about the ▮▮▮▮.
2. She ▮▮▮▮ about the ▮▮▮▮ water.

Review Items

3. When we talk about miles per hour, we tell how ▮▮▮▮ something is moving.

4. Which arrow shows the way the air leaves the balloon?
5. Which arrow shows the way the balloon will move?

6. Tom is 4 miles high. Jack is 20 miles high. Who is colder?

7. Tell why.

8. The arrows show that the temperature is going up on thermometer A and going down on thermometer B. In which picture is the water getting colder, **A** or **B**?

9. In which picture is the water getting hotter, **A** or **B**?

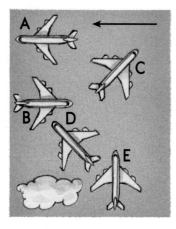

10. Write the letter of the plane in each picture that will go the fastest.

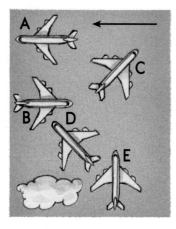

11. The names in one box tell about time. Write the letter of that box.

12. The names in one box tell about length. Write the letter of that box.

A	centimeter inch yard meter mile
B	week year second month minute hour

13. When we weigh very small things, the unit we use is ▮▮▮▮.

14. If you get smaller, your voice gets ▮▮▮▮.

15. Jean got smaller. So what do you know about Jean's voice?

16. Airplanes land at airports. Ships land at ▮▮▮▮.

17. Airplanes are pulled by little trucks. Ships are pulled by ▮▮▮▮.

18. Airplanes unload at gates. Ships unload at ▮▮▮▮.

A

1
1. grocery
2. signaled
3. hinges
4. heavy
5. heavier
6. coast

2
1. remains
2. loss
3. harm
4. squeals
5. groan

B # The Championship Game

Andrew had just received a terrible electric shock. His arm and his neck hurt. But he could tell by the tingling feeling in his feet and hands that he had changed. He was strong again. But he couldn't tell how strong. Was he as strong as an elephant again, or as strong as a small horse? Andrew grabbed the doorknob and squeezed it as hard as he could. He did not dent it. Andrew pulled the door without turning the knob. He tore the door off the hinges. He was strong all right. He was about as strong as a super strong man.

Andy said to himself, "I might not be as strong as I was, but I'm strong enough to help the Titans." He grabbed his jacket and ran from the place he lived. There were many cars on the street. He thought, "I can probably run to the ball park as fast as I could go in a car." So Andy ran.

Nearly everybody in the city could recognize Andy. They had seen pictures of him on TV. There were pictures of him in the windows of grocery stores. People wore large buttons with Andy's picture on them. As Andy ran down the streets toward the ball park, kids of all ages ran along with him. There were big kids and little kids. At first, about twenty kids ran with him. Then the number continued to grow until hundreds of kids followed Andy on the way to the ball park. Crowds gathered along the streets. They cheered. "Andy's going to play," they shouted. Earlier that week, TV news stories had told that perhaps Andy would not play in the championship. The reporters had said that Andy was having some sort of problem and might not play. But when the people saw him running toward the ball park, they knew that he was going to play. "Hooray for Handy Andy," they yelled.

By the time Andy reached the ball park, he was exhausted. He turned around and waved to the boys and girls who had been running with him. He caught his breath and yelled, "We're going to win." They cheered.

Andy ran to the locker room. All the members of the team were on the field. The game had started. Andy could hear the thunder of the crowd. The old man who worked in the locker room said to Andy, "It looks serious. The Wildcats have already scored a touchdown."

Andy struggled into his uniform. He ran out of the locker room and into the ball park. As soon as the fans saw him, they let out a great roar. Andy's muscles were sore from running. He was out of breath. But he was very glad to be on the field. He told himself, "I'm fast and I'm strong. I'll just use my speed and my strength as well as I can."

The coach signaled Andy to kick a field goal. The announcer's voice came over the loudspeakers. "Now playing for the Titans, Handy Andy Dexter."

The crowd went wild. Fans jumped up and down and beat each other on the back. They squealed and shouted and whistled until they almost lost their voices.

Andrew huddled with the other players. The sound of the crowd was so loud that he could hardly hear what they said. Mean George smiled and said, "When I play, you play, right?"

"Right," Andy said.

Andy went back as if he was going to kick the ball. The ball came to him and he started to run. He didn't fool anybody on the Wildcat team. They charged at him and caught him before he could gain anything. First, two Wildcats hit him. Then a third charged into him, helmet first. That was Smiling Sam. His helmet drove right into Andy's ribs. Andy went down and the crowd groaned. Smiling Sam smiled. Then Smiling Sam said, "Hey, little man, you're not going anywhere today except down."

Andy hurt. The Wildcats now had the ball. They moved down the field and scored. They were ahead 14 to 0.

The Titans received the ball and moved up the field. But the Wildcats stopped them. Andy came out to kick the ball. The fans began to clap and stamp their feet.

Andy went into the huddle. "They think I'm going to kick the ball or run with it," Andy said. "I think we can fool them if I throw the ball. I don't think the Wildcats will be ready for a pass."

"Let's try a pass," the other Titans said.

Andy dropped back as if he was going to kick. The ball came to him. The Wildcats charged toward him. Andy dropped the ball.

MORE NEXT TIME

C Number your paper from 1 through 19.

Review Items

Things that are this far apart ←——→ on the map are 2 miles apart.

Things that are this far apart ←————→ on the map are 4 miles apart.

1. How far is it from the park to the hill?
2. How far is it from the forest to the field?

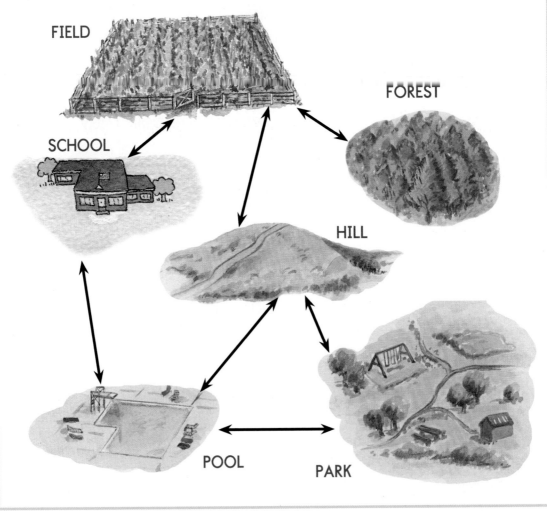

3. You would have the least amount of power if you pushed against one of the handles. Which handle is that?

4. Which handle would give you the most power?

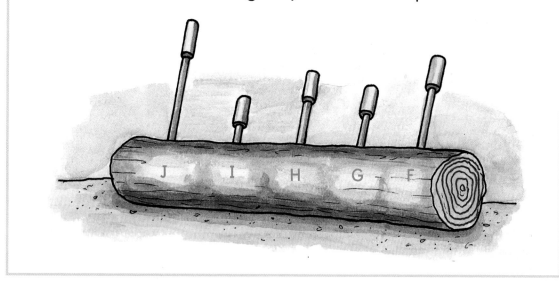

5. The place that is called Troy is now part of what country?
   - Greece   • Turkey   • Italy

6. In what year was the first airplane made?

7. In what year were you born?

8. What year is it now?

9. In what year did the United States become a country?

10. What was the year 2 hundred years ago?

11. What was the year 1 hundred years ago?

12. What was the year 3 hundred years ago?

13. When did the story of Troy take place?

Each statement tells about how far something goes or how fast something goes. Write **how far** or **how fast** for each item.

14. He ran 5 miles per hour.

15. He ran 5 miles.

16. The plane was 500 miles from New York City.

17. The plane was flying 500 miles per hour.

18. Did the first people who lived in caves cook their food?

19. Did the people who lived in caves many years later cook their food?

A

1
1. treasure
2. difficult
3. decision
4. shallow

2
1. <u>eighty</u>
2. <u>guarded</u>
3. <u>remains</u>
4. <u>sunken</u>
5. <u>diver</u>

3
1. before long
2. careful
3. carefully
4. motioned
5. bouncing

4
1. spices
2. loss
3. receive
4. ashamed
5. groan

B

The End of the Game

The ball was on the ground, bouncing around in front of Andy. The Wildcats were charging toward him. There was Smiling Sam, with his helmet down and yelling at Andy, "I got you now."

Andy made himself think. "Use your speed," he told himself. He picked up the ball and then began to run back. The Wildcats couldn't catch him because he was faster than they were. He ran back farther and farther. Then he stopped. For a moment, the crowd was silent. Andy looked down the field, stepped forward, and passed the ball. It was a beautiful pass.

The ball sailed through the air, all the way down the field. The fans were standing. The Wildcats stopped and turned around to watch the ball.

All the Titans except one turned around to watch the ball. That Titan ran. He ran toward the goal. And as he ran, he looked over his shoulder. The ball looked as if it was going to go too far.

But the player made a leap, caught the ball, and slid over the goal line. Touchdown. Andy had just thrown an eighty-yard pass. The Wildcat players were shaking their heads. Andy was smiling. But Smiling Sam wasn't. "You got lucky," he told Andy, and made a mean face.

The Wildcats did not score another touchdown. The Titan players played like champions. They stopped the Wildcats again and again. Late in the game, the Titans scored a field goal. They now had 10 points. The Wildcats had 14 points.

But time was running out. The Wildcats held the ball and moved slowly down the field. They tried to kick a field goal but a Titan player blocked the kick. The score remained at 14 to 10. But now there was less than two minutes left in the game. "Let me go in and try to pass again," Andy said to the coach.

Denny looked at Andy. "Okay, it's your game. Go and win it." Andy ran onto the field. He ran into the huddle. "Let's try another pass," Andy said. Andy dropped back as if he was going to kick the ball. The ball came to him, and he looked for a Titan player to catch the ball. All the players were being guarded by Wildcats. Andy had to try to run with the ball. "I got you now," a mean voice said. CRACK—the sound of a helmet driving into Andy's shoulder pad. He went down for a loss of nearly ten yards. The crowd groaned.

One of the coaches motioned for the team to try a running play. The Titans lined up quickly. Less than a minute remained in the game. The ball went to one of the players who tried to run wide. The Wildcats were waiting. CRACK. Another loss. The clock continued to move.

Denny motioned from the sideline. He wanted the team to try another ⭐ pass. Andy went back. He received the ball. At almost the same time, three Wildcats hit him. Another loss.

The team huddled for the last time. "This is it," Mean George said. "Let's make it a good one."

Andy went back. The crowd was not yelling and whooping anymore. In fact, lots of fans were leaving the stands. The fans thought that the Titans had no chance. The ball came to Andy. He ran back and stopped as if he was going to throw the ball. The Wildcats did not charge after him. They were waiting for the pass. So Andy made a decision: Run. And he ran.

Andy put every bit of strength he had into every step. He ran toward the sideline. He outran every player except one. Smiling Sam was charging toward him. "This is it," Andy told himself. He dropped his shoulder and met Sam's charge. Andy drove with his feet as hard as he could. CRACK.

The people in the stands were standing. Those fans who had started to leave were coming back. They groaned as the football players hit. The fans saw Smiling Sam fly back. Andy managed to keep running, but he had been slowed down. Two Wildcat players were near him. He dodged one and ran over the other. There was one more Wildcat that Andy had to outrun. Andy gave the run everything he had. And he did it. The crowd went wild. The Titans went wild. With only about 10 seconds left in the game, Andy had scored the winning touchdown!

•   •   •

Andy quit playing for the Titans after the championship game. And he never played football again. He lost his super strength. But the Titans gave him a job working with the coaches.

Andy didn't mind losing his strength because he had lived the greatest dream that anybody could have lived. And after that year, he didn't daydream as much. Once in a while he would daydream. But he kept his mind on his job because he really liked his job.

One more thing about Andy: If he goes for a walk, he doesn't walk alone. Before long, a group of kids walks with him. And when they go home, they tell their friends, "Today I was with the greatest football player in the world—Handy Andy."

THE END

C **Number your paper from 1 through 15.**

Review Items

1. What's the boiling temperature of water?

2. Write the letters of the 4 kinds of weapons that soldiers used when they had battles with Troy.
   a. bows　　　b. spears　　　c. planes　　　d. arrows
   e. swords　　　f. rockets　　　g. guns　　　h. tanks

3. During the war with Troy, what did the Greek army build to help them get inside Troy?

4. What was inside this object?

5. What did they do after they came out of the object?

6. Who won the war, Troy or Greece?

7. Name **2** kinds of wells.

8. The temperature inside your body is about ▮▮▮▮ degrees when you are healthy.

9. Most fevers don't go over ▮▮▮▮ degrees.

10. Which letter shows the crude oil?

11. Which letter shows the refinery?

12. Which letter shows the pipeline?

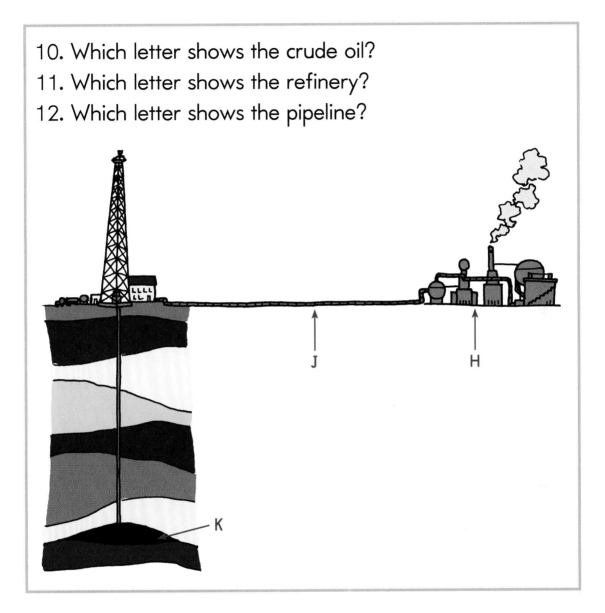

13. How fast is truck **A** going?

14. How fast is truck **B** going?

15. Which truck is going faster?

A

1
1. confusion
2. effort
3. neighbor
4. telephone
5. Hohoboho

2
1. <u>half</u>way
2. <u>some</u>body
3. <u>earth</u>quake
4. <u>flash</u>light

3
1. strangest
2. hardly
3. divers
4. carefully
5. diving
6. lucky

4
1. sunken ship
2. treasures
3. electric
4. shallow
5. difficult
6. mummy

5
1. rich
2. spices
3. noise
4. noisy
5. noisier

6
1. trace
2. cabin
3. sharks
4. worst
5. hooray

B

Places You Have Learned About

In today's story, you're going to read about different places in the world. Make sure that you understand the facts you have learned about the world.

Touch A on map 1. What ocean is that?

Touch B. What country is that? Name two cities in that country.

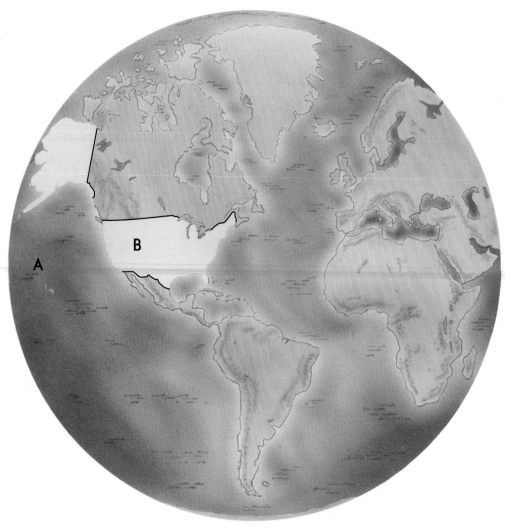

MAP 1

Look at map 2. What is the name of country F? What happened there about 3 thousand years ago?

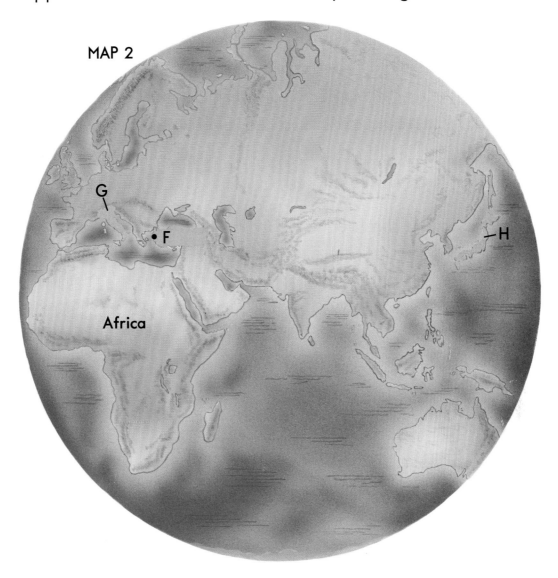

MAP 2

G

• F

Africa

H

What's the name of country G?

What's the name of country H? Name two girls who went to that country.

See if you can find these places on a globe of the world.
- The United States
- Italy
- Turkey
- Japan
- The Pacific Ocean

C Looking for Treasures

Things have changed a lot in the last two hundred years. Two hundred years ago, people traveled from place to place by foot, by horse, or by water.

Two hundred years ago it took a long, long time to go from one place to another. With a good horse, you could travel 30 miles a day. At that speed, it would take you about three months to go from New York to San Francisco. If you fly a jet plane today, it takes far less time to make the same trip.

Ships went across the ocean two hundred years ago, but the ships were not ocean liners like the ones that Linda and Kathy were on.

The ships of two hundred years ago were sailing ships. They had large sails that caught the wind. The faster ships went 6 miles per hour when a good wind was blowing. But the trip from San Francisco to Japan took over 30 days. That is a much longer time than the trip would take in an ocean liner.

The ships of two hundred years ago didn't have refrigerators or electric lights. Rats and insects would often get into the food and ruin it.

Today, the trip from San Francisco to Japan takes only about 5 days, because the ships of today do not use sails. They have large engines. They can move 40 miles per hour.

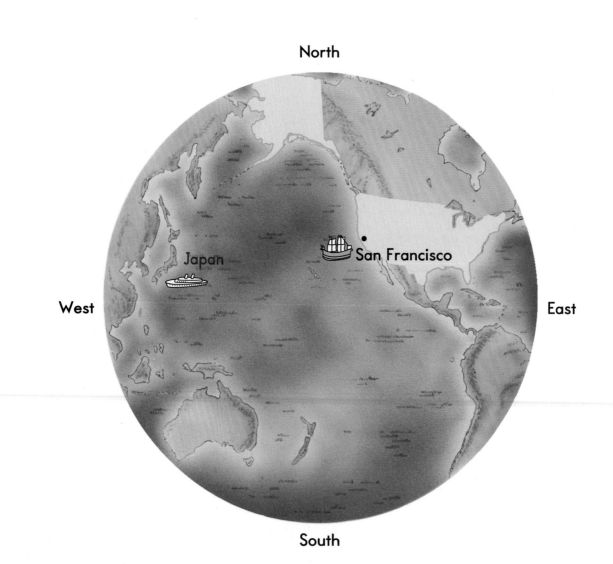

North

West

East

South

Japan

San Francisco

Two hundred years ago, not many ships went between Japan and San Francisco because the trip took so long. But many ships sailed around Italy and Turkey. Ships carried spices, cloth, and things made of gold and silver. Sometimes, ships with great treasures would get caught in a storm. The sails would be torn from the ship. Waves would smash over the ship and it would sink. There are many sunken ships in the oceans around Italy and Turkey.

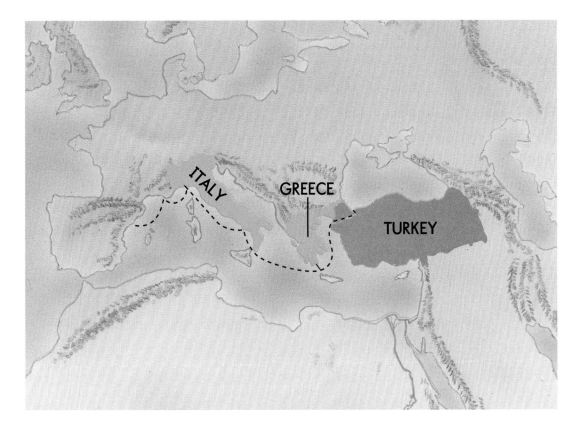

Divers have found some ships that were carrying great treasures. Can you imagine what ⭐ it would be like to find such a ship? You dive for days and days in the blue water, looking for signs of a sunken ship, but you find nothing. The boat that you dive from moves slowly through the sea, trying to trace the path that the sunken ship took when it was on its way to Italy. Parts of the ocean are deep and parts are shallow. You hope that the ship is found in the shallow parts of the ocean, because it is very difficult to dive in the deep parts. Some parts are so deep that you could not go to the bottom without a very special diving outfit.

Day after day, you dive. Then one day, you see something in the shallow water. It looks like part of an old ship. You swim closer and you see that it is an old ship. You go inside it very carefully. You watch out for sharks and strange fish with long teeth. It's dark inside the sunken ship. You swim to the captain's cabin. Then you see the treasure—boxes with locks on them. Inside are gold coins—piles of them. You are rich.

But not many divers who look for sunken ships are as lucky as you are.

Things have changed a lot in the past two hundred years. The trip from New York to Italy would have taken 14 days by sailing ship two hundred years ago. But today, we can go to the airport in New York, get on a jet, and be in Italy 7 hours later. We can call on the phone from New York and tell somebody in Italy that we will be there at 3 o'clock. We can order diving equipment by phone. When we get off the plane in Italy, we can take a cab to the harbor. We can then rent a boat and begin our search for sunken treasure.

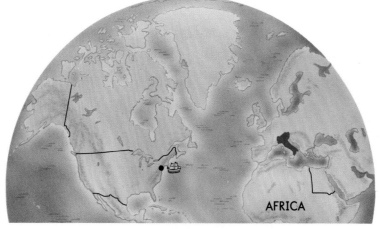

AFRICA

THE END

D Number your paper from 1 through 16.

Review Items

1. Which letter shows where the ground gets warm first?
2. Which letter shows where the ground gets warm last?

3. In which season is the danger of forest fires greatest?
4. What do people keep in banks?

Some of the lines in the box are one inch long and some are one centimeter long.

5. Write the letter of every line that is one centimeter long.

6. Write the letter of every line that is one inch long.

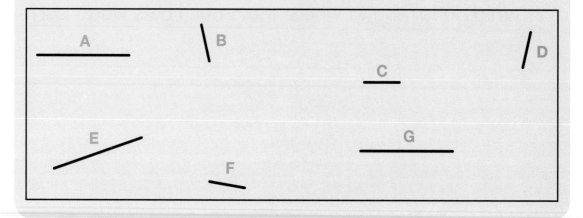

7. Greece went to war with Troy because of a woman named ▨▨.

8. The woman from Greece was important because she was a ▨▨.

9. The woman from Greece went away with a man from ▨▨.

10. What's a good place to look for clues about people who lived long ago?

11. Some people who lived 80 thousand years ago lived in ▨▨.

12. When we dig into the pile in the picture, what's the first thing we find?

13. What's the next thing we find?

14. What's the next thing we find?

15. What's the next thing we find?

16. What's the last thing we find?

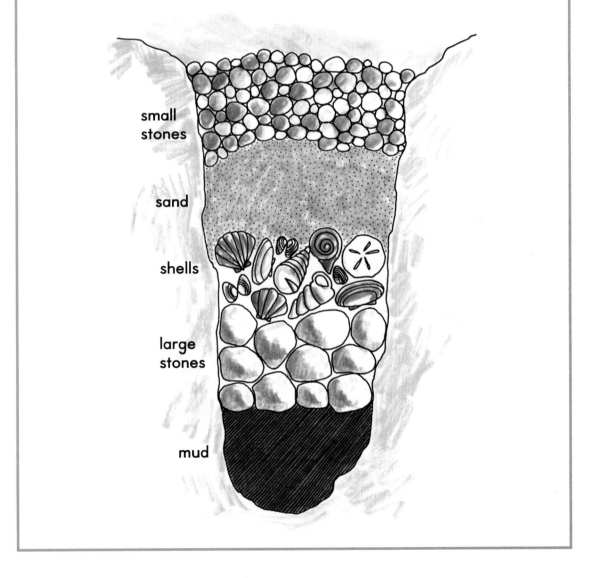

small
stones

sand

shells

large
stones

mud

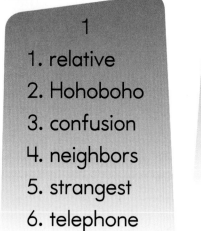

A

1	2	3
1. relative	1. worst	1. noisier
2. Hohoboho	2. wonder	2. rather
3. confusion	3. wander	3. happy
4. neighbors	4. world	4. happiest
5. strangest		5. effort
6. telephone		6. hooray

B

Words That Talk

You're going to read a story about words that talk. The picture shows some of those words. The words are saying things to each other.

What is the word **hot** saying?

What is **cold** saying?

Who is **cold** talking to?

What is **worry** saying?

Who is saying, "Everybody, take it easy"?

Calm is trying to keep things calm.

C   Hohoboho

This is a story about a sad word that lived in a make-believe place called Hohoboho. The words in Hohoboho were not like the words in our world. And the people in Hohoboho were not like the people in our world. These people talked, but they didn't do anything else. The people didn't read. They didn't play baseball. They didn't eat. They didn't even sing. All they did was talk.

Here's the strangest part about Hohoboho. Every time a person said a word, that word felt happy.

Words that were said a lot were very, very, happy.

Words that were said quite a bit were happy part of the time.

Words that were said only once in a while were sort of sad.

The rest of the words were very sad.

How often did people say words that were very sad?

The word in our story was hardly ever said. So you know how that word felt.

All words in Hohoboho stayed in a strange place called the word bank. There were over one hundred rows in the word bank.

Here are the rules about where the words sat in the word bank: **The words that people said more often sat near the front of the word bank. The words that people didn't say very much sat near the back of the word bank.**

The happiest words sat in the front rows of the word bank.

Every time somebody said a word, that word would jump up and yell, "I'm the best," or "Hooray for me." Here are some of the words that ⭐ sat in the best seats of the word bank: **me, am, what, who, is, we, I, not.** These are words people say all the time. They say the word **me** and the word **you.** They say the word **here** and the word **there.** They say the word **have** and the word **had.** Name some other words that people say a lot.

Words that were sort of happy sat in the middle rows of the word bank. These words were said quite a bit but not as often as words like **you** and **how.** Here are some words that sat in the middle: **should, other, telephone, rather.** These words didn't yell and shout all day long. But they were a lot noisier than the words in the back. Every now and then one of the words in the middle of the word bank would jump up and say, "That's me."

With all the yelling and shouting, the word bank was very loud.

Which part of the bank was the loudest?

Which part was sort of loud?

Which part was pretty quiet?

The back of the bank was so quiet that a whole day might pass without one sound from the back of the bank.

The words that sat near the back of the word bank were words that you wouldn't say very often. Here are some words that sat near the back: **confusion, fifteenth, mummy.** Name some other words that sat near the back of the word bank.

You'll never guess which words sat in the very last rows of the word bank.

MORE NEXT TIME

D Number your paper from 1 through 13.

Review Items

1. What part of the world is shown on the map?
2. The map shows how far apart some places are. How far is it from **G** to **F?**
3. How far is it from **C** to **D?**

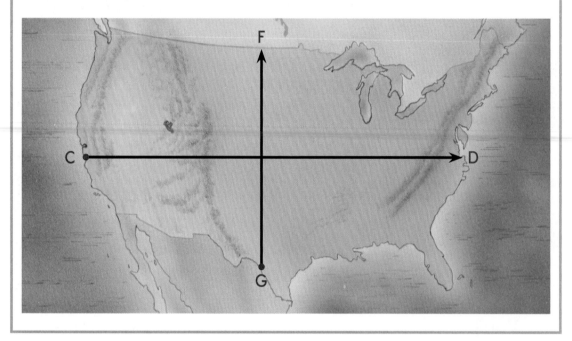

4. Find **F** on map 1. What place does the **F** show?

5. What place does the **E** show?

6. Find **C** on map 2. What place does the **C** show?

7. What happened in place **C** about 3 thousand years ago?

8. What's the name of place **D**?

9. What's the name of place **B**?

10. What's the name of place **A**?

Map 1   **Map 2**

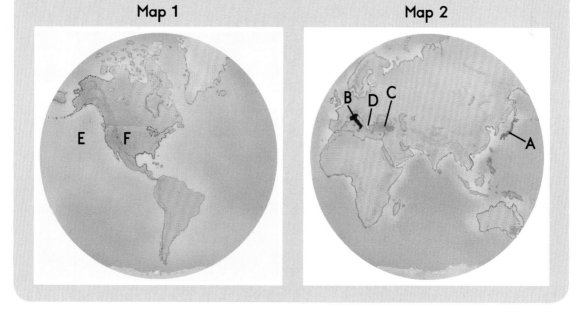

11. How fast is car **A** going?

12. How fast is car **B** going?

13. Which car is going faster?

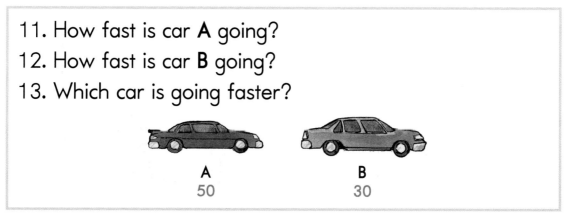

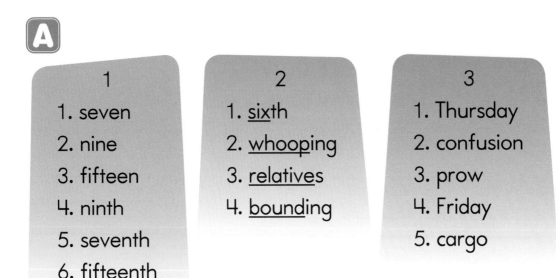

A

1	2	3
1. seven	1. <u>sixth</u>	1. Thursday
2. nine	2. <u>whooping</u>	2. confusion
3. fifteen	3. <u>relatives</u>	3. prow
4. ninth	4. <u>bounding</u>	4. Friday
5. seventh		5. cargo
6. fifteenth		

B

Liz Takes a Trip

Liz liked cool weather. It was the middle of summer, and she wanted to go to a city in California that was cool in the summer. So she went to the city of ▮▮▮▮.

Liz knew that the temperature of an object tells how ▮▮▮▮ that object is. When she left New York City, the air on the ground was 30 degrees. When the plane went higher and higher, did the air outside the plane get hotter or colder?

The plane flew much faster than a car can go. How fast did the plane fly?

When the plane went from New York City to San Francisco, it was going in which direction?

The plane was facing the wind, so the name of the wind was a ▮▮▮▮.

Did the plane go faster or slower than a plane going in the opposite direction?

The air that rushed from the jet engines was going to the east, so the jet engines moved toward the ██████. The jet engines were attached to parts of the plane. Those parts were the ██████.

As Liz flew along, she wanted to get a good look at things on the ground below. So she looked through something that makes things look very big. She looked through ██████. She saw the city that was between Chicago and Salt Lake City. What city was that?

In San Francisco, Liz saw a lot of animals at a zoo. She knew how much some of the animals weigh.

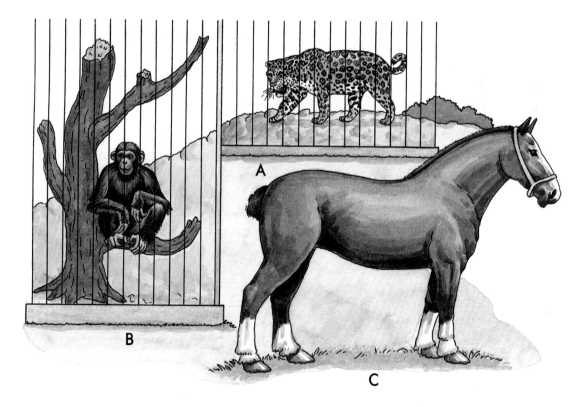

C The Words That Sat in the Back Rows

The words that sat in the back of the word bank didn't have much fun. They tried not to listen to the other words yelling and cheering, but they couldn't help it. They wanted to be said more often. Every now and then one of the words in front would turn around and say something like, "Look at those words in the back of the bank. They aren't any good at all."

One word that sat in the very last row of the word bank was the word **run.**

If we had a word bank in our world, the word **run** would not sit in the back row. The word **run** would be said very often because people run and talk about running. But you must remember that the people in Hohoboho did not do anything. So they didn't talk much about doing things. They didn't talk about running or jumping or walking. You know other things they didn't talk about very much.

So the word **run** sat in the last row. The word **run** sat behind words like **speedometer** and **temperature.** The word **run** sat behind words like **maggots, enough, binoculars,** and **direction. Run** sat next to its relatives. One relative was the word **runner.** Another relative was the word **ran.** You know some of the other relatives of **run.**

Next to the **run** family sat the **walk** family. You know some of the relatives of **walk** that were in that family. And next to that family was the **jump** family, and then the **ride** family, and the **eat** family.

Every once in a while, one of the words from the back row would try to sit closer to the front of the word bank. Look at the picture. Two words are sitting in the wrong seats.

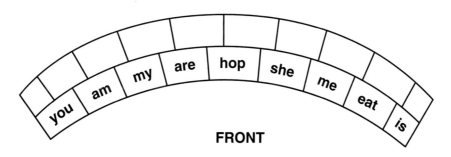

FRONT

This trick didn't work because the other words always caught the words from the back row. "Hey, you can't move up here," they would say. "Go back to the last row where you belong." So the sad words would sit and wait and hope. Once in a while, somebody would say their names and they would feel good, very good. They tried to remember how good they felt. Sometimes, they would talk about it. The word **runner** liked to say, "I remember one day when my name was said four times. Four times in one day."

The other sad words got tired of hearing this story. They would say, "Oh, be quiet. You just got lucky. You usually don't have your name said once a month."

"Yeah," one of the other sad words would say. "You don't get said any more often than the rest of us."

"It will happen again," **runner** would reply. "You'll see. One of these days, they're going to start saying my name all the time. I'll bet I get to move up five rows. You'll see."

"Oh, be quiet."

Then the sad words would sit back and feel sad. Long day after long day, they would sit and try not to listen to those words in the front of the bank whooping and howling.

MORE NEXT TIME

D Number your paper from 1 through 18.

Skill Items

Their amazing effort surprised the neighbors.

1. What word names people who live near you?
2. What word means **strength?**
3. What word means that something is hard to believe?

Review Items

4. Write the letter of the tree that has deeper roots.
5. Write the letter of the tree that begins to grow first every year.

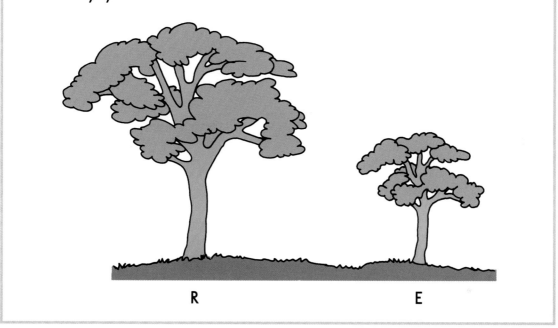

R   E

6. Which letter shows the crude oil?

7. Which letter shows the fresh water?

8. Which letter shows the salt water?

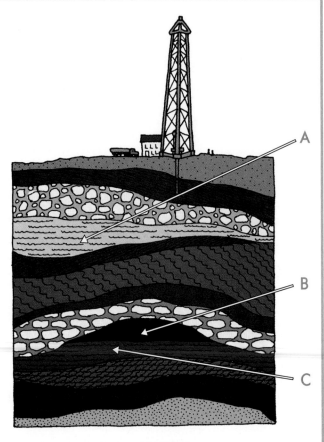

9. Gasoline comes from a liquid called ▬▬.

10. When was the check below written?

11. Who should the bank pay?

12. How much should the bank pay?

13. Whose money should the bank use to pay Lee Butler?

June 3, 2001

Pay to _Lee Butler_ $ 12.00

Twelve dollars

Yoko Tanaka

14. Name 2 things that a strong magnet can pick up.

15. How many parts does the body of an insect have?

16. How many legs does an insect have?

17. How many legs does a spider have?

18. How many parts does a spider's body have?

Number your paper from 1 through 18.

1. Find **A** on map 1. What place does the **A** show?
2. What place does the **B** show?
3. Find **C** on map 2. What place does the **C** show?
4. What happened in place **C** about 3 thousand years ago?
5. What's the name of place **D**?
6. What's the name of place **E**?

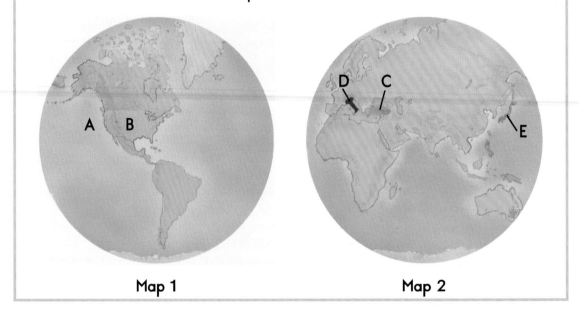

Map 1   Map 2

7. Write the letters of 3 ways that people traveled 2 hundred years ago.

        a. by jet   d. by walking
        b. by water   e. by horse
        c. by train   f. by car

8. Write the letters of all the words that belong to the **jump** family.

9. Write the letters of all the words that belong to the **ride** family.

a. ride	f. rider	k. chair	p. flying
b. jumping	g. sitting	l. jumper	q. riding
c. hot	h. talked	m. hiding	r. eats
d. book	i. jumps	n. see	s. jump
e. rode	j. rides	o. jumped	t. run

Skill Items

For each item, write the underlined word from the sentences in the box.

> She <u>commented</u> about the <u>still</u> water.
> Their <u>amazing</u> <u>effort</u> surprised the <u>neighbors</u>.

10. What underlining means **quickly told about something?**

11. What underlining names people who live near you?

12. What underlining means that something is hard to believe?

13. What underlining means **silent** or **peaceful?**

14. What underlining means **strength?**

END OF TEST 11

Lesson 110   **71**

A

1
1. officer
2. police
3. Friday
4. cargo

2
1. happy
2. fifteenth
3. happier
4. sixth

3
1. squeeze
2. tumble
3. stumble
4. seventh
5. stumbled

4
1. ninth
2. begin
3. beginner
4. Thursday
5. confusion

B

Facts About Canada

You have learned about the United States. The United States is not a city and not a state. What is it?

The United States is one of the largest countries in the world, but the country that is just north of the United States is much larger. That country is Canada.

Alaska touches the west side of Canada. The rest of the United States touches the south side of Canada.

Alaska

Canada

United States

C The Big Change in Hohoboho

Every Friday, words in the word bank were moved. Sometimes the people in Hohoboho started to say a word more often. On Friday, that word would be moved closer to the front of the word bank.

The opposite also happened. If a word was not said as often as it had been said, it was moved toward the back of the word bank. A lot of words would be moved around every Friday, but they were usually moved only one or two rows. The word **eraser** was usually in the sixth row, but every now and then it would move up as far as the fourth row or as far back as the ninth row.

When **eraser** was in the ninth row, it felt quite sad. But the words in the very back row would give anything to be able to sit in the ninth row. The ninth row was near the front of the bank. In fact, it was so close to the front of the bank that **run** couldn't even see it.

Anyhow, words got moved around every Friday, and the words that moved up cheered and shouted. The words that got moved toward the back didn't act the same way. The word that got moved the most rows was **summer. Summer** once went from the fifteenth row to the seventh row.

Summer didn't stay in the seventh row very long. The move to the seventh row happened during the summer when the weather got very hot. People talked a lot about summer. Then the weather cooled down, and **summer** got moved back to the fifteenth row.

As you know, words were always ✦ moved on Friday. But one Thursday, a big change took place, and the entire word bank was thrown into confusion. Here's what happened. The people in Hohoboho began to **do** things. The people began to swim and walk and eat and run. They began to look at things, kick things, and sit on things. They began to wonder, and sing, and dance. The people talked about the things they did. So the whooping and hollering in the word bank now came from a different part of the bank. "Let's dance," the people in Hohoboho would say, and a great cry went out from one of the rows.

"That's me," a word shouted.

"Dancing is fun," another person would say, and one of the relatives of **dance** would jump up. "That's me. People are talking about me."

Things were crazy in the word bank. The words in the front of the bank turned around and looked and listened. They couldn't believe what was happening. There was still some shouting and yelling from the front of the word bank, but there was much more noise from the back of the bank. The words in the back were so happy that they were jumping and howling and bounding all over the place.

"Twenty times," the word **hop** said. "They said my name twenty times and the day isn't even over yet."

"That's nothing," **run** said, "I'm already up to 56."

Two words in the front row, **we** and **us,** were talking. **We** said, "Tomorrow is Friday. What do you think will happen to those words in the back row?"

"I don't know," **us** said. "We'll have to wait and see."

MORE NEXT TIME

 Number your paper from 1 through 26.

Skill Items

Use the words in the box to write complete sentences.

effort	noticed	neighbors	still	awful
world	commented	special	amazing	

1. She ▮▮▮ about the ▮▮▮ water.
2. Their ▮▮▮ ▮▮▮ surprised the ▮▮▮.

Review Items

Write what kind of horse each picture shows.

- Mongolian horse
- draft horse
- pony
- racehorse
- quarter horse

3.

4.

5.

6.

7.

8. Which animal is safer, a cow or a cat?

9. Why?

10. Electricity can turn any steel bar into a magnet. What are these magnets called?

11. Name a place where these magnets are used.

Write the name of each part of a football player's uniform.

- shoulders
- shoulder pads
- knee pads
- helmet
- hats

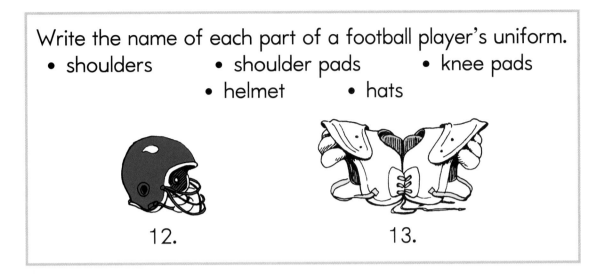

12.

13.

14. Which stopwatch shows that 3 seconds have passed?

15. Which stopwatch shows that 9 seconds have passed?

16. Which stopwatch shows that 5 seconds have passed?

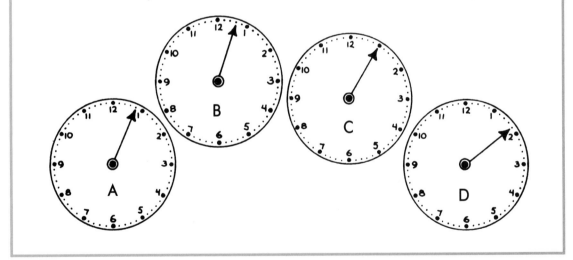

17. If the hang-time for a kick is 2 seconds, how long does the ball stay in the air?

Some of Andrew's hang-times are shown on the stopwatches.

18. Write the letter of the watch that shows his best hang-time.

19. How many seconds are shown on that watch?

20. Write the letter of the watch that shows his worst hang-time.

21. How many seconds are shown on that watch?

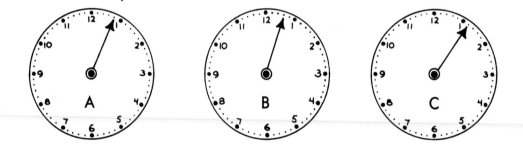

22. Write the letters of 3 relatives of the word **sit**.
a. sits   b. talked   c. sat   d. hopped   e. walker   f. sitter

23. Eohippus lived ▓▓▓▓ million years ago.

24. The front legs of eohippus were different from the front legs of a horse that lives today. Write the letters of 2 ways that they were different.
a. They had smaller hooves.   b. They didn't have hooves.
c. They were faster.   d. They were smaller.

25. Write the letter of the shortest hang-time.
26. Write the letter of the longest hang-time.
a. 8 seconds   b. 4 seconds   c. 6 seconds   d. 5 seconds

A

1
1. double
2. Australia
3. kangaroo
4. squeezed

2
1. stumbled
2. beginner
3. finest
4. breathed
5. dusty
6. stomping

3
1. complete
2. notice
3. happier
4. easy
5. easier
6. officer

4
1. cloud
2. Toby
3. police
4. drunk
5. silent
6. joey

B

Run Gets Moved

It was the day that the words in the word bank got moved.

Here's how the words got moved every week. A voice would make the announcements about which words were to move. For example, the voice would say, **"Telephone** moves to row six." How would the voice announce that **me** has to sit in row three?

If a word was named in an announcement, the word would have to go to a new seat. The word would have to keep that seat until the voice announced that the word was to move again.

The announcements in the word bank were made at 9:00 in the morning on Fridays. The announcements were usually over by 9:30. But on the Friday after the big change, all the words knew that things would be different. They knew that a lot of announcements would be made. The words like **me** and **are** were interested in what would happen to those words in the back row. **Me** and **are** were so interested that they did not do much yelling and shouting when the people in Hohoboho said their names.

The words in the back row had been so happy that they were tired of yelling and shouting and feeling good. **Run** said to **walk,** "I don't really care if they move me or not. I feel great."

"Me, too," the other word said.

At 9:00 the announcements began, and they were not finished until late at night. Nearly every word in the word bank was moved. Sometimes whole rows of words were moved. And some words moved more than 100 rows. The most amazing announcement of the day came about 10:30 in the morning after two or three hundred words had been moved. Here was that announcement: "The words **run** and **walk** will move from row 110 to row 1."

For a moment the word bank was  silent. Some words turned to their neighbors and said, "Did that announcement say that **run** and **walk** will move to row 1?"

Run looked over at **walk.** They just stared at each other. Then they stood up and started to walk to the front row. Suddenly the words in the back row began to clap for them. Then they began to cheer.

"That's my relative," the word **walking** said. "That word used to sit right next to me."

There are only so many seats in each row. Two new words were moved to row one. So you know what had to happen to two words that were already in row one. The word **were** and the word **only** moved to row two. They were very mad.

Run sat in the seat that **were** had used. **Run** was next to some relatives of **were** who were still in the first row. One word was **are. Are** turned to **run** and said, "They'll probably move you back next week."

Run laughed and said, "I don't care. I'll remember this forever. This is great."

By the end of that Friday, **run** could turn around and talk to some of its relatives that were in row two. The words **running, runs,** and **ran** were in row 2. **Runner** was in row five, but **runner** was very happy. "I never thought I would even see this part of the word bank," **runner** said.

When the next Friday came around, the words like **run** and **walk** and **jump** and the others kept their seats near the front of the word bank. In fact, they're still there. And **run** is no longer sad. In fact, **run** is happy all day and all night. **Run** yells and shouts and says, "That's me. I'm number one." And the other words that had been in the last row are happier than they ever thought they would be.

THE END

C Number your paper from 1 through 18.

Skill Item

1. Compare object A and object B. Remember, first tell how they're the same. Then tell how they're different.

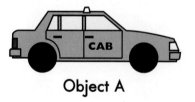

Object A

Object B

Review Items

2. What is the name of the vehicle in the picture?
3. How many wheels does the vehicle have?
4. What is pulling the vehicle?
5. What is soldier A doing?
6. What is soldier B doing?

Soldier A

Soldier B

7. The country to the north of the United States is ▮▮▮▮.
8. Is the United States **bigger** than most other countries or **smaller** than most other countries?
9. Which country is bigger, Japan or the United States?
10. Which country is bigger, the United States or Canada?

Write what kind of horse each picture shows.

- racehorse
- quarter horse
- pony
- Mongolian horse
- draft horse

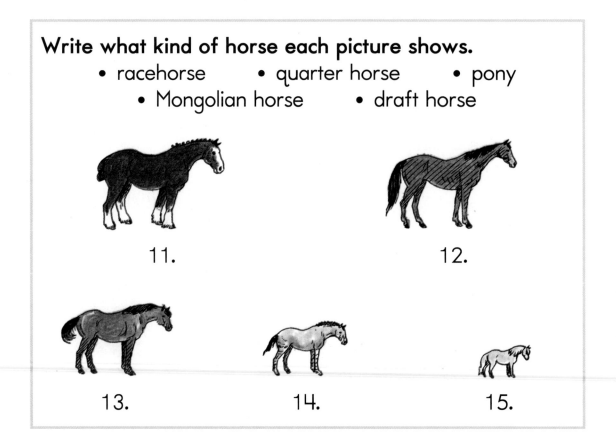

11.

12.

13.

14.

15.

16. What place does the **A** show?
17. What place does the **B** show?
18. What place does the **C** show?

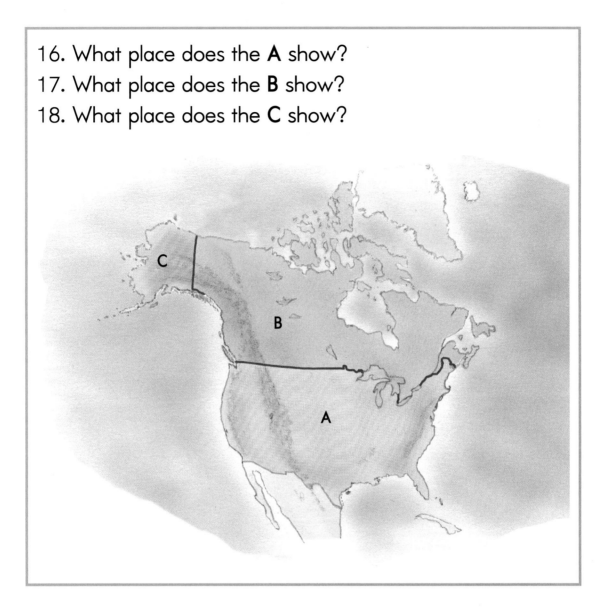

A

1	2	3
1. finest	1. triple	1. kangaroo
2. breathed	2. Australia	2. joey
3. dusty	3. cloud	3. herd
4. ashamed	4. double	4. drunk
5. dancing	5. Toby	5. stomping
6. soundly	6. refers	6. carries

B   ## Facts About Australia

The story that you will read today begins in Australia.
The map shows that the United States and Canada are on

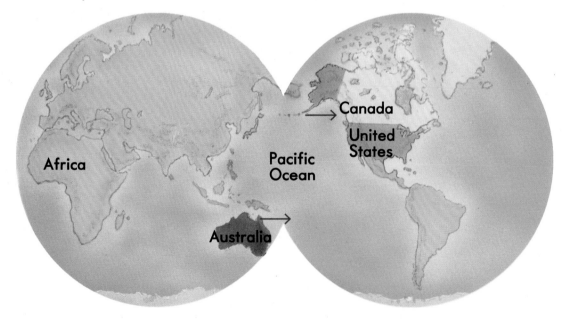

one side of the world. Australia is on the other side of the world.

Touch the United States.

Touch Canada.

Touch Australia.

Touch the United States again. Now go west from the United States.

What's the name of the ocean you go through when you go west from the United States?

The ocean that is west of the United States is the same ocean that is east of Australia.

Many animals that live in Australia do not live in any other place in the world. You can find some of these animals in zoos, but the only place you can find them living as wild animals is Australia.

Below are some animals that live in Australia.

platypus

kangaroo

koala

C Toby the Kangaroo

This story starts in Australia, where Toby lived. Toby was a kangaroo. Like other kangaroos, he was part of a mob. A mob is a herd of kangaroos. There were over 50 kangaroos in Toby's mob.

Toby's mob was not the biggest mob in Australia and it was not the smallest, but it was like the other mobs in one way: It moved around from place to place. Every year, the mob would move in a great circle. The mob would stay in a place for a while, until the kangaroos had eaten the grass or drunk the water holes dry. Then the mob would hop, hop, hop to the next place where there was grass and water.

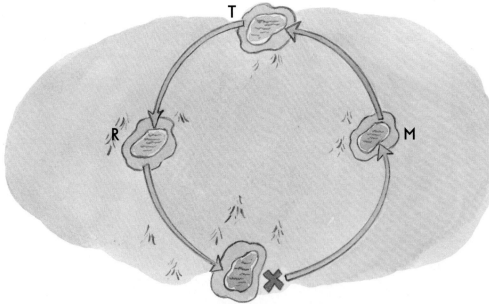

Those 50 kangaroos hop, hop, hopped on ground that was dry and dusty. Those kangaroos made a cloud of dust that you could see for many miles. When the ground was

very, very dry, the leader of the mob would be the first to hop along. Just behind the leader would be other kangaroos that were important in the mob. The kangaroos that were right behind the leader were more important than the kangaroos that came after them.

The leader did not have to breathe any dust. The important kangaroos that came right after the leader had to breathe a little bit of dust. The kangaroos that were not very important to the mob came last, right in the middle of the dust.

Toby was the last kangaroo in the whole mob. Toby breathed lots and lots of dust. When the leader said that the mob was going to move to another place, some of the kangaroos would cheer. Toby ★ did not cheer. He would say things like, "Oh, bad, double bad, and big bad."

If you looked at Toby, you might wonder why he was the very last kangaroo. He was a fine-looking kangaroo. He was strong. And he had the finest tail of any kangaroo in the mob. He was nearly as big as the biggest kangaroo in the mob, but Toby was just a boy kangaroo. The other kangaroos looked at Toby and said, "He is a fine-looking kangaroo. Too bad he's a joey."

A kangaroo does not like to be called a joey. A joey is a baby kangaroo. So when you call a big boy kangaroo a joey, you are calling him a big baby. Toby sure didn't like to be called a joey, but Toby was a big baby. He didn't work. He was always saying things like, "Bad, double bad, big bad." The only two things he liked to do were eat and sleep. He could eat faster than anything you've ever seen eat. And he could sleep so soundly that he wouldn't wake up if the mob was singing and dancing and stomping all around him.

So Toby had to stay near the back of the mob as he hopped along and breathed dust. He kept mumbling, "Oh, double and triple bad." When the mob stopped for a rest, Toby had to listen to the other kangaroos call him a joey. Even Toby's mother was ashamed of him. She liked him, but she wished that he would grow up and stop being a joey. She did not know that very soon Toby would save the mob from kangaroo hunters.

MORE NEXT TIME

D **Number your paper from 1 through 26.**

1. Which letter shows where Australia is?
2. Which letter shows where the United States is?
3. Which letter shows where Canada is?
4. Which letter shows where the Pacific Ocean is?

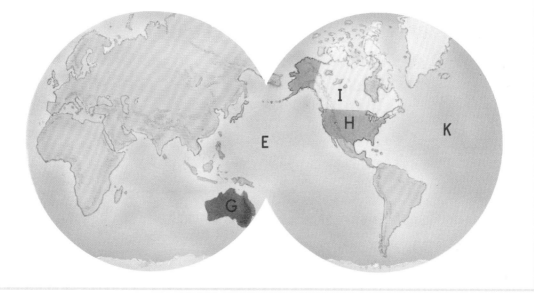

5. Which letter shows a kangaroo?
6. Which letter shows a platypus?
7. Which letter shows a koala?

Police officers checked the ship's cargo.

8. What words mean **cops**?

9. What word refers to the things that a ship carries?

Review Items

10. Jean is 16 miles high. Sue is 8 miles high. Who is colder?

11. Tell why.

12. Write 2 letters that show bulkheads.

13. Write 2 letters that show decks.

14. Which letter shows where the bow is?

15. Which letter shows where the stern is?

16. What is the temperature of the water in each jar?

17. Write the letter of each jar that is filled with ocean water.

18. Jar E is not filled with ocean water. How do you know?

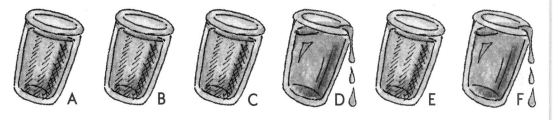

19. Write the letter of the one name that tells about temperature.

20. Write the letters of the 6 names that tell about distance or length.

21. Write the letters of the 5 names that tell about time.

22. Write the letters of the 2 names that tell about speed.

    a. meters per week   h. miles
    b. years   i. meters
    c. inches   j. days
    d. minutes   k. centimeters
    e. feet   l. miles per hour
    f. degrees   m. hours
    g. weeks   n. yards

23. Three thousand years ago, part of Greece went to war with ████.

24. The war began because a queen from ████ ran away with a man from ████.

25. ████ ships went to war with Troy.
   - 5 thousand
   - 1 thousand
   - 1 hundred

26. How long did the war last?

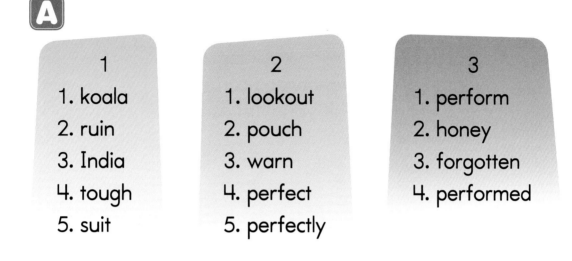

A

1	2	3
1. koala	1. lookout	1. perform
2. ruin	2. pouch	2. honey
3. India	3. warn	3. forgotten
4. tough	4. perfect	4. performed
5. suit	5. perfectly	

B   ## Facts About Kangaroos

Here are facts about kangaroos:
- There are many different kinds of kangaroos. Some kangaroos are as big as a man. Other full-grown kangaroos are not much bigger than a rabbit.
- When a kangaroo is born, it is only three centimeters long.

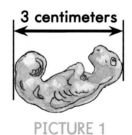

3 centimeters

PICTURE 1

- The baby kangaroo lives in its mother's pouch for half a year.
- Kangaroos have strong back legs and strong tails. In one jump, bigger kangaroos can jump over 10 feet. If a big kangaroo hit you with its tail, it would knock you down.

PICTURE 2

 A Job for Toby

Toby was called a joey. Toby had to hop along through the dust at the back of the mob. And there were only two things that Toby really liked to do.

Just after the sun came up one day, the leader of the mob hopped over to where Toby was sleeping. The leader hit the ground with his tail. He hit it so hard that it made a thump you could hear two miles away. Although Toby could sleep through nearly anything, he woke up. The leader looked at him and said, "The time has come for you to stop being a joey. Today you are going to be a lookout." Then the leader asked, "Do you know what a lookout does?"

Toby said, "A lookout looks out for trouble." Toby was a little frightened. This was the first time the leader had spoken to him.

The leader said, "And what does a lookout do if there is trouble?"

Toby blinked. Then he said, "Smack your foot on the ground so that it makes a big noise."

"You are right," the leader said. Then the leader continued, "Go to the top of that hill and look out for a couple of hours. Then the mob will start moving."

🌼 Toby looked at the hill the leader pointed to. It was a very big hill. Toby was thinking about how hard it was going to be to climb to the top of that hill. But he didn't say anything, except, "Okay."

As Toby started up the hill, his mother hopped up to him. "Be careful, honey," she said. "Remember what happened to your ✦ father."

"Oh, bad and big bad," Toby mumbled. He had almost forgotten about his father.

Years ago, when Toby was just a tiny kangaroo in his mother's pouch, Toby's father was a lookout. But he fell asleep ❀ and hunters caught him. Nobody in the mob ever saw his father again. But some of the kangaroos heard that he had been taken from Australia to another country, far across the Pacific Ocean. He was supposed to be in some kind of circus in that country.

Toby remembered his father. His father had the longest tail that any kangaroo ever had. And Toby's father had three large white spots on the top of his tail. Toby would never forget such a fine tail.

So Toby continued up the hill. He was getting so tired that he could hardly mumble, "Double, double bad." Finally, he reached the top, where he caught his breath. The sun was bright. The air was clear. There was no dust. When Toby sat down, he didn't mean to fall asleep, but he did. Toby really wanted to be a good lookout. He wanted to show the other kangaroos that he was not a big, lazy joey. But with the bright sun shining down, and that soft grass under him, he just rolled over, closed his eyes, and . . . zzzzzzzzz . . . zzzzzzzzz . . . . He was snoring away.

For a while, he was having a nice dream. Then he heard a voice in his dream. The voice said, "Don't wake that lookout. He'll warn the others." Suddenly, Toby realized that the voice was not part of a dream. He opened his eyes and looked around. Five hunters were sneaking past him on their way down the hill to the mob.

MORE NEXT TIME

D Number your paper from 1 through 21.

Skill Items

1. Compare object A and object B. Remember, first tell how they're the same. Then tell how they're different.

Object A

Object B

Use the words in the box to write complete sentences.

| neighbors | cargo | flight attendants | police officers |
| puzzled | effort | dashboard | amazing | double |

2. Their ▮▮▮▮ ▮▮▮▮ surprised the ▮▮▮▮.
3. ▮▮▮▮ checked the ship's ▮▮▮▮.

Review Items

4. During the war between part of Greece and Troy, what kept the soldiers from getting inside Troy?
5. At last, the Greek army built a ▮▮▮▮.
6. What was inside this object?
7. What did the men do at night?

8. **Write the letters** of the 9 places that are in the United States.

a. Australia   g. Lake Michigan   m. San Francisco
b. New York City   h. Japan   n. California
c. Chicago   i. Turkey   o. Canada
d. Alaska   j. Texas   p. Denver
e. China   k. Italy
f. Ohio   l. Greece

9. If you go east from Australia, what ocean do you go through?
10. If you go west from the United States, what ocean do you go through?
11. What is a group of kangaroos called?
12. What is a baby kangaroo called?

13. Write the letters of the 5 lines that are one inch long.

14. Write the letters of the 5 lines that are one centimeter long.

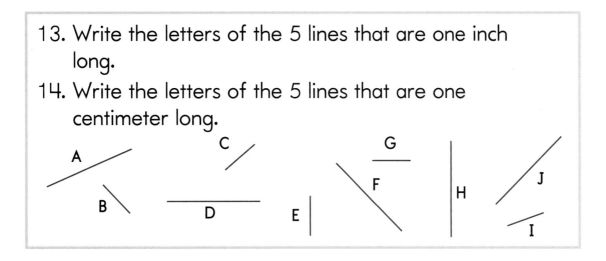

15. Which letter shows where Australia is?

16. Which letter shows where the United States is?

17. Which letter shows where Canada is?

18. Which letter shows where the Pacific Ocean is?

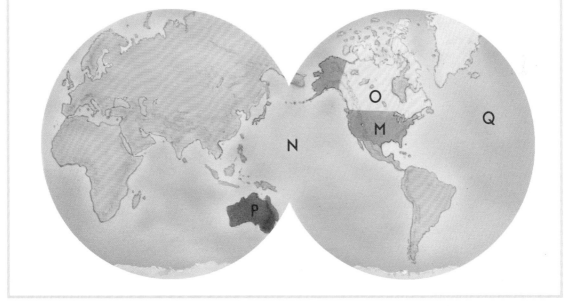

19. Which is longer, a yard or a meter?

20. Which is longer, a centimeter or a meter?

21. How many centimeters long is a meter?

115

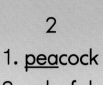

A

1
1. feather
2. spread
3. heading

2
1. <u>pea</u>cock
2. <u>color</u>ful
3. <u>sail</u>ors
4. <u>sig</u>naled
5. <u>tack</u>led

3
1. screeches
2. dark-colored
3. ruin
4. tough
5. performed

4
1. Mabel
2. koalas
3. suit
4. argued
5. perfectly

B **Facts About** Peacocks

You will read about a peacock in the next lesson.
Here are facts about peacocks:

- A peacock is a large bird. A full-grown peacock is two meters long from its head to the end of its tail.
- The feathers of the male peacock are more colorful than the feathers of any other bird. When the male peacock shows off, it spreads out its tail feathers.
- The peacock is not a wild bird of Australia.
- The peacock has a very unpleasant voice. The peacock does not sing. It screeches.

C The Kangaroo Hunters

Toby woke up and saw five kangaroo hunters. The leader was named Mabel. She was tough and nobody argued with her, not even the captain. The captain was the captain of a ship that was waiting about ten miles from Toby and the mob. The captain's sailor suit was too big for him and he kept pulling his pants up. The other three hunters were sailors from the ship.

Mabel ran a large circus in Canada. She was on a trip around the world to get animals—lots of them. She came to Australia to get kangaroos and koalas. She didn't plan to use all the animals that she caught. She planned to sell many of them to zoos or other circuses. She would keep the best animals.

When Mabel saw the mob down at the bottom of the hill, she knew that she was close to some very good animals. She sat down in the tall grass next to the captain. She whispered, "There's a big, dark kangaroo down there. We must get her."

"Yeah," the captain said in a loud voice.

"Be quiet," Mabel whispered. "If you wake up that lookout, you'll ruin everything."

"Oh, yeah," the captain said in a whisper and turned around to see if Toby was still sleeping. He seemed to be sleeping, but he wasn't. He was listening to everything Mabel and the captain were saying. He was pretending to be asleep because he didn't know what else to do. He didn't want to slam his foot against the ground because he was afraid that the hunters might shoot him. He didn't want to be shot.

"Come on," Mabel said as she put her binoculars away. "Let's sneak down this hill and get behind the mob. We should be able to catch at least five kangaroos before they know we're around. Let's just make sure that we get that big, dark-colored one."

"Yeah, let's go," the captain said, and signaled his men to follow Mabel down the hill.

So there was Toby, pretending to be asleep as the hunters started to sneak down the hill. Below him was the mob. As Toby watched the hunters move down the hill, he said to himself, "Oh, great big bad. I can't let those hunters take kangaroos from my mob." Toby sat up. He lifted his foot into the air and he brought it down with a terrible smack. The sound echoed through the hills. For a moment, every kangaroo in the mob stood still, without moving and without breathing. Again, Toby signaled—smack.

This time, the kangaroos moved. And did they ever move fast. They all took off in the same direction at full speed. They made a cloud of dust that you could see all the way back at the captain's ship.

"Run, jump, get away from those hunters," Toby shouted as he smacked his foot against the ground again.

Mabel stood up, turned around, and looked at Toby. Then she shouted, "Well, there is <u>one</u> kangaroo that is not going to get away."

"Yeah, that's <u>right</u>," the captain hollered in a mean voice. The captain and Mabel were looking right at Toby.

"Oh, triple bad," Toby said to himself and started to hop down the other side of the hill. He went fast, but one of the sailors went faster than Toby went. By the time Toby reached the bottom of the hill, that sailor was right behind him. With a great leap, Toby tried to get away. With a greater leap, the sailor tackled Toby.

"We <u>got</u> him," Mabel yelled.

"Yeah," the captain said.

MORE NEXT TIME

D Number your paper from 1 through 21.

Skill Items

Write the word from the box that means the same thing
as the underlined part of each sentence.

important	although	confused	foul
motioning	constructing	opposite	normal

1. They finished <u>building</u> the house last week.
2. The garbage smelled <u>bad</u>.
3. She went to school, <u>but</u> she was sick.

4. Compare the word **two** and the word **to**. Remember,
   first tell how they're the same. Then tell how they're
   different.

Review Items

5. In what year did the United States become a country?
6. What is the only country that has wild kangaroos?
7. How far can a kangaroo go in one jump?
8. A kangaroo is ▮▮▮▮ centimeters long when it is born.
9. Big kangaroos grow to be as big as a ▮▮▮▮.

10. Which letter shows a kangaroo?

11. Which letter shows a platypus?

12. Which letter shows a koala?

13. Where does a baby kangaroo live right after it is born?

14. How long does it live there?

15. Toby's father had a tail that was different from any other kangaroo's tail. Name 2 ways that his father's tail was different.

16. What part of a car tells how fast the car is moving?

17. When a plane flies from New York City to San Francisco, is it flying in the **same direction** or the **opposite direction** as the wind?

18. Which thing went into the pile earlier, thing **R** or thing **X**?

19. Which thing went into the pile earlier, thing **J** or thing **T**?

20. Which thing went into the pile later, thing **R** or thing **T**?

21. Which thing went into the pile later, thing **Y** or thing **J**?

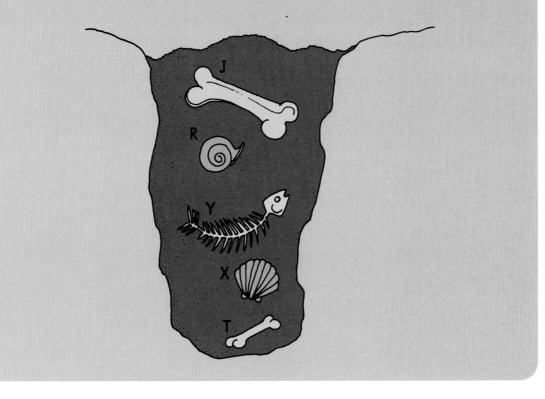

A

1

1. preserve
2. strutted
3. ramp
4. India
5. rainbow
6. aren't

B **Facts About Minutes**

Today's story tells that Toby's eyes got used to the dark after a few minutes went by.

Here are facts about minutes:

- There are 60 seconds in a minute. If you count slowly to 60, one minute will go by.

- Some clocks have a hand that moves fast. When that hand goes all the way around the clock, one minute goes by.

C　Facts About Ships

In today's story, you will read about a ship. The picture shows the parts of a ship.

Ships carry things from place to place. Ships may carry grain or cars or machines. These things are called the **cargo.** A ship that carries grain has a cargo of grain.

The cargo is carried in a part of the ship called the **hold.** The hold is at the bottom of the ship.

D　Toby on the Ship

Toby was in a cage, hanging from a long pole. Two sailors were carrying the pole—one at each end. Toby bounced up and down as the sailors walked. Next to them, the captain moved along, pulling up his pants every few steps. Mabel led the group. "Come on," she would holler from time to time. "Let's get moving."

"Yeah, get moving," the captain would say.

By the time Toby reached the ship, the sun was in the west. Toby hoped the sailors would let him out of the cage now. He said, "Oh, large and terrible bad," as he bounced along.

"Be <u>quiet</u>," Mabel yelled. The sailors carried Toby up the ramp and across the deck of the ship. The sailors put Toby's cage in front of a doorway that led down to the hold of the ship. Mabel yelled, "Put that kangaroo into the hold."

"Yeah," the captain said. "Into the hold."

The two sailors opened the door to the hold and tossed Toby down the stairs. It was so dark inside the hold that Toby couldn't see a thing at first. He looked to the left and looked to the right. He could smell other animals, but he couldn't see a thing.

Then, after a few minutes, his eyes got used to the dark and he could see the other animals. He could see three kangaroos and he could see something else. It was beautiful. Even in the dim light, its feathers shined like a rainbow. It was the biggest, most beautiful peacock you have ever seen.

The peacock puffed itself up. "Aren't I beautiful?" the peacock said. "Even in this terrible place, I am lovely, aren't I?"

"Oh, bad," Toby said to himself.

The peacock kept talking. "I'll bet that you felt bad when they threw you in here, but I know that you're happy now that you can see me. I was worth waiting for, wasn't I?"

"Oh, double bad," Toby said.

"Don't you just <u>love</u> my colors?" the peacock continued. "Of course, everybody knows that my tail feathers are the most beautiful things in the world, but look at some of my other feathers."

The peacock strutted out into the middle of the hold, where there was some sunlight that came through a crack. "If you want to see beauty, just take a look at these." The peacock turned around three times.

"Oh, triple bad," Toby said.

"Don't listen to that turkey," one of the other kangaroos said. The kangaroo continued, "That peacock will drive you nuts."

The peacock said, "I am <u>not</u> a turkey. I am the bird of India, the most beautiful thing in the world. I am not plain looking, like you animals from Australia."

Toby didn't want to talk about beautiful birds. He said, "When do we eat around here?"

The peacock said, "We get fed once a day. That won't happen until the sun goes all the way down, so you can still look at my feathers for a little while. That's better than eating anyhow."

"Oh, double bad," Toby said to himself. Then he turned to the other kangaroos and said, "Does anybody know where this ship is taking us?"

The peacock said, "I know and I'll tell you as soon as I show you something that you will remember forever." The bird puffed up and turned around very fast in the sunlight. Then he said, "Wasn't that something?"

Toby still didn't want to talk about beautiful birds. He said, "Where are we going?"

"I'll give you a clue," the peacock said. "The country we're going to is just north of the United States."

Toby said, "I don't know the name of that country."

The peacock said, "My, you animals from Australia don't know much. The country that is just north of the United States is Canada."

MORE NEXT TIME

E **Number your paper from 1 through 19.**

Skill Items

Here's a rule: **Every plant is a living thing.**

1. A duck is not a plant. So what else do you know about a duck?

2. An oak tree is a plant. So what else do you know about an oak tree?

3. A boy is not a plant. So what else do you know about a boy?

4. Compare object A and object B. Remember, first tell how they're the same. Then tell how they're different.

Object B

Object A

Review Items

5. A kangaroo that sits on a hill and warns the mob when trouble is coming is called a ___.
6. What's the name of the large, beautiful bird of India with a colorful tail?
7. How many meters long is that bird from its head to the end of its tail?
8. What does a male peacock spread when it shows off?
9. Which is more beautiful, a peacock's feathers or a peacock's voice?
10. A kangaroo is ___ centimeters long when it is born.
11. Big kangaroos grow to be as big as a ___.
12. Where does a baby kangaroo live right after it is born?
13. How long does it live there?

Write **W** for warm-blooded animals and **C** for cold-blooded animals.

14. beetle

15. cow

16. horse

17. spider

18. bee

19. The people who lived in caves drew pictures on the cave walls. Write the letters of 4 things they made pictures of.

a. hands   e. horses

b. fish   f. cows

c. bears   g. birds

d. dogs   h. elephants

A

1	2	3	4
1. certain	1. <u>ca</u>mera	1. breaking	1. field
2. surprise	2. <u>foot</u>steps	2. liars	2. law
3. imagine	3. <u>blank</u>ets	3. crossed	3. untied
4. recognize	4. <u>interest</u>ing	4. heading	4. entertain
	5. <u>pre</u>serve	5. wiggling	

B

The End of the Trip

The ship was on its way to Canada. The peacock told the others that the trip would take ten days. "But don't worry," the peacock added, "I'll entertain you for the trip. You'll have a lovely time."

"Big and double big bad," Toby said to himself.

But before the trip was over, Toby had become friends with the peacock. The peacock's name was Pip. And Toby learned a lot from Pip. Pip knew the name of the ocean that the ship crossed. Toby had never heard of the Pacific Ocean before. Pip also knew a lot about the captain and Mabel.

On the day before the ship reached Canada, Pip told Toby, "Mabel and the captain are crooks. When you were in Australia, you lived on a game preserve. It's against the law to hunt on a game preserve."

"Oh, that's double bad," Toby said.

Pip said, "Mabel and the captain are also liars. They pretended that they were going to take my picture with a camera. Mabel told me to stand in the middle of a field so that I would be in the bright sun."

Pip continued, "Then Mabel told me that the captain should stand behind me. That seemed like a good idea. The captain is so ugly that I would look twice as beautiful with him behind me. How did I know that he would drop a net over me?"

Toby mumbled to himself, "Not bad."

The ship was supposed to dock in Canada the next day. There was a little hole in the side of the hold. The animals took turns looking out of this hole, trying to see the shore. Pip was looking through the hole just after noon. "My, my," he said suddenly. "I don't see the shore, but I do see something that is very interesting." ⭐

"What's that?" the other animals asked.

"I'll give you a clue. This thing goes through the water. It carries police officers. And it's probably looking for ships that are breaking the law."

Toby pushed the peacock out of the way and looked through the hole. He saw a police boat. And the boat was heading right toward their ship.

"We're saved," Toby shouted. "The police have caught Mabel and the captain."

"Not quite," the peacock said. "You'll discover that Mabel is very smart, even if she is a <u>crook</u>."

Two sailors ran into the hold. The sailors slapped tape over the mouth of each animal. Then they quickly tied up the animals and covered them with large blankets. Then they dumped a pile of sacks on top of the animals.

Toby said to himself, "Very, very bad."

Toby could hear people talking near the doorway to the hold.

"What do you want, Officer?" Mabel said in a sweet voice.

"We're supposed to look at your cargo," the officer said.

"As you can see," Mabel said, "we're just carrying sacks of grain."

"Yeah," the captain said. "Sacks of grain."

Footsteps moved into the hold. Toby tried to make some sound by wiggling around.

The officer said, "Sounds as if you have rats in here. Better be careful or they'll get into your grain."

"Thank you, Officer," Mabel said. "We'll take care of the rats."

"Yeah," another voice said. "We'll take care of the rats."

Then the footsteps moved up the stairs. There was the sound of a door closing. A minute or two later, there was the sound of a motor that moved farther and farther from the ship Toby was on.

When one of the sailors untied the animals, Pip said, "What did I tell you? Mabel may be a crook, but she is very smart."

Things looked bad for Toby.

MORE NEXT TIME

C Number your paper from 1 through 21.

Skill Items

> **The champions performed perfectly.**
> 1. What word means **without any mistakes?**
> 2. What word means **put on a show?**
> 3. What word means they won the championship?

Review Items

4. If you go east from Australia, what ocean do you go through?

5. What does a male peacock spread when it shows off?

6. Which is more beautiful, a peacock's feathers or a peacock's voice?

7. What is a group of kangaroos called?

8. What is a baby kangaroo called?

9. Which letter shows the stern?

10. Which letter shows the hold?

11. Which letter shows a deck?

12. Which letter shows the bow?

13. Which letter shows a bulkhead?

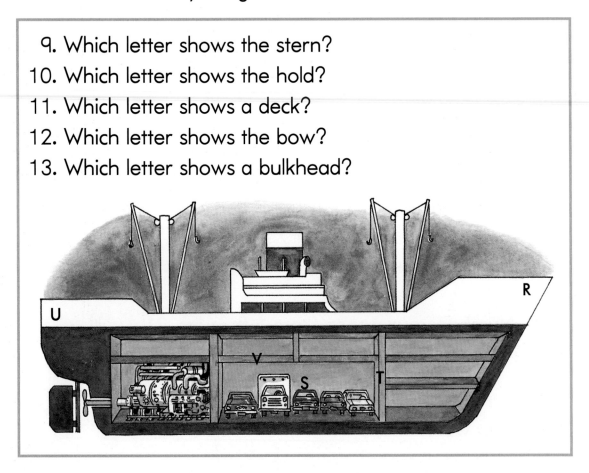

14. What do we call the part of a ship where the cargo is carried?

15. Name the country that is just north of the United States.

16. How many seconds are in one minute?

17. Some clocks have a hand that moves fast. When that hand goes all the way around the clock, how much time has passed?

18. The hand that moves fast went around 6 times. How much time passed?

19. A mile is more than ▮▮▮▮ feet.

20. Things closer to the bottom of the pile went into the pile ▮▮▮▮.

21. Things closer to the top of the pile went into the pile ▮▮▮▮.

A

1	2	3	4
1. amount	1. <u>i</u>llegal	1. <u>road</u>side	1. graph
2. correct	2. <u>scold</u>ing	2. <u>worth</u>less	2. sped
3. thumping	3. <u>a</u>wake	3. <u>foot</u>steps	3. pleasant
4. recognize	4. <u>can</u>non	4. <u>gentle</u>man	4. arrives

B   More Facts About Canada

In the story you'll read today, Toby arrives in Canada. You've learned facts about Canada. Which is larger, the United States or Canada?

Is Canada **north** of the United States or **south** of the United States?

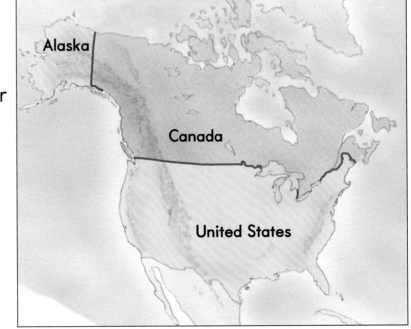

Here are two new facts about Canada:
- Canada is colder than the United States.
- Far more people live in the United States than live in Canada. The graph compares the number of people who live in the United States and Canada.

This bar shows how many people live in Canada.

This bar shows how many people live in the United States.

C The Ship Arrives in Canada

When the ship docked in Canada, it was night. Toby had been sleeping. He heard the sound of footsteps coming down the stairs to the hold. As Toby rubbed his eyes and tried to wake up, he realized that Pip was talking. Pip said, "I'll bet that they're going to try to sneak us into trucks and get us out of here before the police find out that there is illegal cargo on this ship."

Before Toby was completely awake, the three sailors had moved all the other animals from the hold. Toby was the last to go. He could hear Pip on the top deck, scolding the sailors. "Be careful with my feathers. Don't you recognize beauty when you see it?"

Three sailors started down the stairs for Toby. One of them tripped and fell into the other two. All three sailors fell into the hold. They began yelling at each other.

While the sailors yelled, Toby started to sneak up the stairs.

Just then, a loud voice from the top of the stairs said, "Throw a net over that kangaroo, you fools."

A moment later, a net fell over Toby. He tried to free himself, but he couldn't. The sailors hauled him up the stairs and dumped him onto a cart. "Take that kangaroo down the ramp," a voice yelled.

"Yeah, down the ramp," another voice said.

A sailor started to push the cart down the ramp. Part of the net got caught under the sailor's foot. The sailor

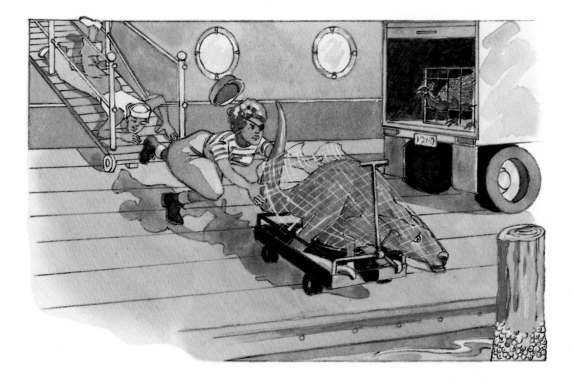

tripped and fell forward. When he fell forward, he let go of the cart. The cart sped down the ramp. The cart continued to speed across the dock. It sped past a truck with the other animals in it. As Toby went by the truck, he could hear Pip saying, "Have a pleasant trip."

Toby's trip was not very pleasant. The cart came to the end of the dock, where there was a large post. The cart hit the post and sent Toby flying through the air. Toby flew right over the post. But the net caught on the top of the post and left Toby hanging above the water.

"Get that kangaroo," a voice hollered, and Toby could hear footsteps thumping down the dock. Then Toby felt the net being pulled up onto the dock. The sailors carried him to the truck with the other animals. Pip was saying, "Now be careful about my feathers. Don't push against me."

"Oh, triple bad," Toby said.

While it was still dark outside, the truck went to a circus. "This is where you get off," Mabel said to Toby. "You are going to be one of the stars of this tiny circus. You'll entertain people by being shot from a great cannon."

"Oh, <u>many</u> kinds of bad," Toby said.

The circus owner put a chain around Toby's neck and led him to a cage. Toby waved goodbye to Pip and the other animals. The circus owner told Toby, "Tomorrow, you will be a star. You will do tricks for people."

Toby didn't want to do tricks. He did not want to live in a cage and work for a circus. He wanted to be back home in Australia. As he sat there in that dark cage, he thought about the dust. The dust didn't seem very bad to him now. He missed the thumping sound of the mob. He missed the leader. Toby missed his mother and the other kangaroos. He missed the smell of grass and the sound of the wind.

As he sat there in his cage, he felt a large tear run down the side of his nose and fall off. "Oh, very bad," he said to himself and tried to go to sleep. Poor Toby even missed Pip.

MORE NEXT TIME

D Number your paper from 1 through 23.

Skill Items

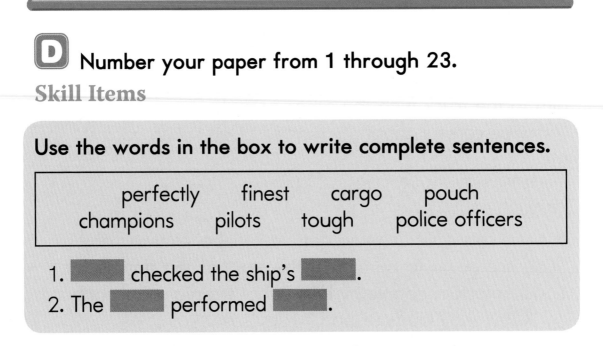

Use the words in the box to write complete sentences.

| perfectly | finest | cargo | pouch |
| champions | pilots | tough | police officers |

1. ▭ checked the ship's ▭.
2. The ▭ performed ▭.

Review Items

Write the letter that shows where each place is.

      3. Italy   7. Canada

      4. Greece   8. United States

      5. Turkey   9. New York City

      6. San Francisco

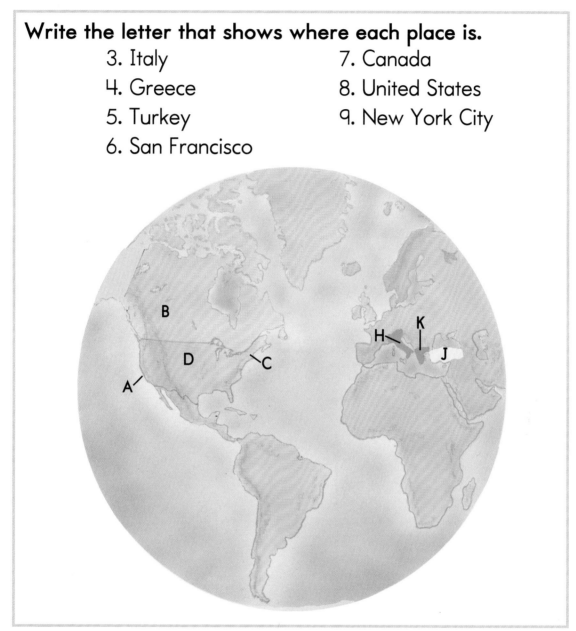

10. What is the only country that has wild kangaroos?

11. How far can a kangaroo go in one jump?

12. A kangaroo is ▇▇▇ centimeters long when it is born.

13. Big kangaroos grow to be as big as a ▇▇▇.

14. Where does a baby kangaroo live right after it is born?

15. How long does it live there?

16. How many seconds are in one minute?

17. Some clocks have a hand that moves fast. When that hand goes all the way around the clock, how much time has passed?

18. The hand that moves fast went around 8 times. How much time passed?

For items 19–23, write the correct years.

• 1985   • 1982   • 1987   • 1981   • 1989

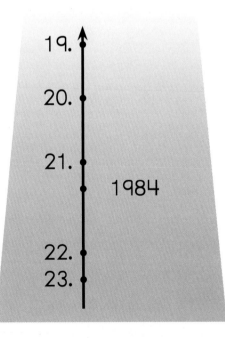

19.

20.

21.

1984

22.

23.

A

1	2
1. <u>per</u>form	1. correct
2. <u>pre</u>sents	2. rip-off
3. <u>rather</u>	3. complaining
4. <u>um</u>brella	4. worse
5. <u>shab</u>by	5. amount

B

Facts About a Circus

In today's lesson, you're going to read about a circus that is not very good. People enjoy a good circus.

Here are some facts about a good circus:

- The circus is sometimes held in a large tent. The picture shows a huge circus tent.

• Two or three acts go on at the same time in a large circus. Some of the acts are on the ground. Other acts take place high in the air.

The favorite acts on the ground are trained animals and clowns. People like to see lions, tigers, and elephants do tricks.

The favorite acts in the air are people diving from one swing to another swing or people walking on wires.

A

B

Ⓒ Toby's New Job

The next morning, the circus owner came and took Toby from his cage. The owner said, "You are going to do tricks for the people who have come to see our circus. If you want to eat, you will do tricks. If you do <u>not</u> do tricks, you will become a <u>very</u> hungry animal."

Toby said, "Oh, bad and super bad."

The owner took Toby into a tent. In the middle of the tent was a ring.

"What a shabby circus," Toby said to himself.

This circus did not have many animals and people doing super things. Toby was the only animal in the tent. The owner was dressed up in a black suit with a rip in the back of the coat.

There was no huge crowd of people watching the act. There were about twenty people sitting in the stands. Three of them were sleeping. Two of them were little kids who were crying. The rest of them were complaining.

One girl said, "We want to see lions and tigers."

"Yeah," somebody else said. "We don't want to see a dumb kangaroo."

The owner held up his hands. "This kangaroo can do tricks that will surprise you. This kangaroo is the smartest kangaroo in the world. People usually pay as much as a hundred dollars to see this kangaroo perform."

"Boo," the people yelled. "We want lions."

Then a girl yelled, "Make that kangaroo ride a bicycle."

"Make him ride it backward," a boy yelled.

The other people began to clap. "Yes, let's see him ride a bicycle backward."

"Wouldn't you rather see him being shot from a cannon?" the owner asked.

"No," the people agreed. "We want to see that kangaroo ride a bicycle backward."

🌼 The owner tried to argue with the crowd, but when people started to throw things at him, he said, "All right, he will ⭐ ride a bicycle backward."

The owner got a dusty bicycle. He held up one hand and said to the crowd, "Ladies and gentlemen. Today the Kankan Circus presents Toby, the wonder kangaroo. Toby will amaze you by riding a bicycle backward. And he will do this amazing trick on a high wire ten meters above the floor.

Toby looked up at the wire ten meters above the floor. You know what Toby said.

The owner handed Toby 🌼 the bicycle and said, "Take this bicycle up the ladder. Then ride it backward on the high wire."

Toby shook his head, no.

The owner said, "<u>Do</u> it, you bad kangaroo. Get up there and ride that bicycle."

Toby shook his head, no.

The owner turned to the crowd. "Before Toby, the wonder kangaroo, rides the bicycle on the high wire, he will ride it backward on the floor." The owner turned to Toby. "Ride that bicycle on the floor."

Toby shook his head, no.

People were beginning to throw things at Toby and the owner. "This is a rip-off," they were hollering. "That kangaroo can't do anything."

The owner said, "One moment, ladies and gentlemen. Before Toby rides the bicycle backward on the floor, Toby will ride it forward on the floor."

The owner looked at Toby and said, "Do it." Toby shook his head, no.

People were now yelling, "I want my money back," and "Let's call a cop."

The owner held up his hands and said, "Before Toby rides the bicycle forward on the floor, Toby will walk with the bicycle on the floor."

Toby looked at the owner and shook his head no again.

"This is the worst show in the world," people were yelling. A woman was shaking her umbrella at the owner. Two boys were throwing papers at Toby. Toby was saying, "Oh, worse than bad."

MORE NEXT TIME

D **Number your paper from 1 through 21.**

Review Items

1. Which direction would you go to get **from Canada** to the main part of the United States?

2. Which country is **smaller,** Canada or the United States?

3. Which country is **colder,** Canada or the United States?

4. Where do **more** people live, in Canada or in the United States?

5. Which letter shows Canada?

6. Which letter shows the United States?

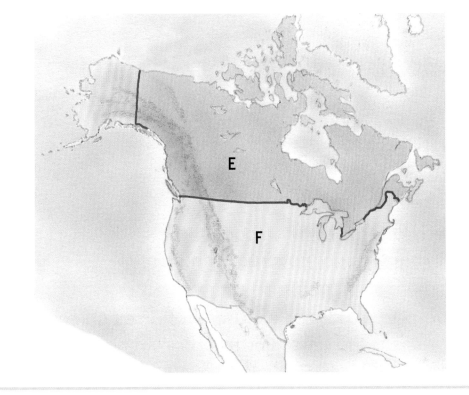

7. Tom is 4 miles high. Jack is 20 miles high. Who is colder?

8. Tell why.

9. What year is it now?

10. In what year were you born?

11. In what year was the first airplane made?

12. What was the year 1 hundred years ago?

13. What was the year 2 hundred years ago?

14. In what year did the United States become a country?

15. What was the year 3 hundred years ago?

16. During a storm, which comes first, lightning or thunder?

17. How does fire like to move, up or down?

18. The picture shows the outline of a hand on a cave wall. Which letter shows the part of the wall that was covered with paint?

19. Which letter shows the part of the wall that was not covered with paint?

20. Cave people painted pictures of horses on cave walls. How are those horses different from horses that live today?

21. Which horse has a shorter back, a racehorse or a quarter horse?

Number your paper from 1 through 32.

1. Which direction would you go to get from the main part of the United States to Canada?

2. Which country is **larger,** Canada or the United States?

3. Which country is **warmer,** Canada or the United States?

4. Where do **more** people live, in Canada or in the United States?

5. Is the United States **bigger** than most other countries or **smaller** than most other countries?

6. In what country are peacocks wild animals?

7. What is the only country that has wild kangaroos?

8. How far can a kangaroo go in one jump?

9. A kangaroo is ▮▮▮ centimeters long when it is born.

10. Where does a baby kangaroo live right after it is born?

11. How long does it live there?
    • half a month   • half a year   • half a week

12. What place does the **A** show?

13. What place does the **S** show?

14. What place does the **J** show?

15. What place does the **Z** show?

16. What place does the **P** show?

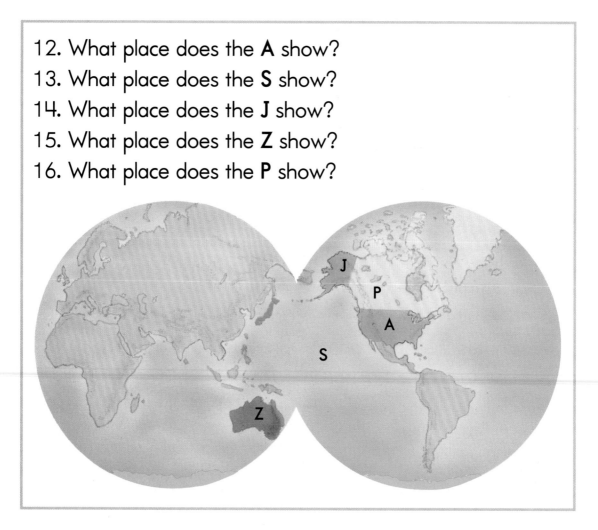

17. What's the name of the large, beautiful bird of India with a colorful tail?

18. How long is that bird from its head to the end of its tail?

19. What is a group of kangaroos called?

20. What is a baby kangaroo called?

21. How many seconds are in one minute?

22. Some clocks have a hand that moves fast. When that hand goes all the way around the clock, how much time has passed?

23. The hand that moves fast went around 8 times. How much time passed?

24. If you go east from Australia, what ocean do you go through?

Skill Items

For each item, write the underlined word or words from the sentences in the box.

<u>Police officers</u> checked the ship's <u>cargo</u>.
The <u>champions</u> <u>performed</u> <u>perfectly</u>.

25. What underlining means **put on a show?**

26. What underlining means **cops?**

27. What underlining refers to the things that a ship carries?

28. What underlining means **without any mistakes?**

29. What underlining means they won the championship?

Here are three things you did as part of the test:
- a. You answered questions about animals.
- b. You answered items about Canada and the United States.
- c. You answered questions about the meanings of words.

30. Write the letter of the thing you did near the beginning of the test.
31. Write the letter of the thing you did near the middle of the test.
32. Write the letter of the thing you did near the end of the test.

END OF TEST 12

A

1

1. encyclopedia
2. hallelujah
3. truth
4. homonym

2

1. <u>re</u>funded
2. <u>work</u>er
3. <u>per</u>haps
4. <u>loud</u>ly
5. <u>re</u>ply

3

1. certain
2. roadside
3. stupid
4. boxer
5. amount

4

1. worthless
2. gloves
3. mountains
4. wear

B **Facts About** Boxing

The story in the next lesson will tell about kangaroos boxing. Here are facts about boxing:

- Two people box.
- The boxers wear large mittens called boxing gloves.
- The boxers box inside a place that is roped off. Although this place is not round, it is called a ring.
- The boxers hit each other with the gloves.

Mabel said, "Imagine. We sold him that worthless kangaroo for one thousand dollars. Then we bought him back for one hundred dollars. Not bad."

"Yeah," the captain said. "Not bad."

Mabel said, "Now we'll sell that kangaroo to the Roadside Zoo for one thousand dollars and we'll make more money."

"Yeah," the captain said. "More money."

The truck left the city and drove for hours into the mountains. Then it stopped. Toby saw a sign, "Roadside Zoo." Toby saw other signs: "Amazing Animals," "Killer Snakes," "Apes," and "The Beautiful Bird of India." A worker was putting up a ⭐ new sign. It said, "Boxing Kangaroos."

One of the sailors led Toby into this zoo. The zoo smelled very bad. It wasn't the kind of zoo that has many animals. There were about ten animals. Each was in a small cage. One of them was talking very loudly. "How in the world can I entertain people if I don't even have enough room to spread out my lovely feathers?"

"Pip," Toby hollered.

But Toby didn't have a chance to talk with Pip. The sailor led Toby to the end cage, far from Pip. There was already another animal in this cage. It was a kangaroo—a big one. The sailor shoved Toby into the cage.

In the distance, Mabel was saying, "And now you have two boxing kangaroos."

It was very crowded in that small cage. There were legs and tails all over the place. Toby could see two tails. One of them was very big. Along the top of that tail were three white spots. Toby looked at the tail and counted the spots. Then he looked at the kangaroo. There was only one kangaroo in the whole world that had a tail like that. "Daddy," Toby said. "Daddy."

For a moment, the large kangaroo stared at Toby. Then he said, "Are you my little Toby?"

"Yes, Daddy," Toby said. "It's me. They caught me and brought me here."

"Oh, son," Toby's father said, with a tear running down the side of his nose. "I am so glad to see you."

The two kangaroos hugged each other with their short little front legs. Then they talked. They talked about dust and blue skies and the mob and Australia. They talked about Toby's mother and the leader and the other kangaroos from the mob. Then Toby's father said, "Son, we've got to get out of this terrible place and go home."

Toby said, "Double good."

MORE NEXT TIME

D Number your paper from 1 through 19.

Skill Items

Here are 3 events that happened in the story. Write **beginning, middle,** or **end** for each event.

1. Mabel and the captain took Toby to the Roadside Zoo.
2. Toby recognized his father.
3. The owner talked to Mabel on the phone.

She paid the correct amount.

4. What word tells how much there is?
5. What word means **right?**

Review Items

6. Write the letters of the 5 names that tell about time.
7. Write the letter of the one name that tells about temperature.
8. Write the letters of the 6 names that tell about distance or length.
9. Write the letters of the 3 names that tell about speed.

a. degrees	f. hours	k. miles per year
b. minutes	g. weeks	l. yards
c. miles per hour	h. centimeters	m. years
d. meters	i. miles	n. inches per week
e. inches	j. days	o. feet

10. You can see drops of water on grass early in the morning. What are those drops called?
11. When we weigh very small things, the unit we use is ______.
12. Name **2** kinds of wells.
13. Gasoline comes from a liquid called ______.

14. The arrow that killed Achilles hit him in the ▇▇▇▇.

15. That arrow had something on it that killed Achilles. What did it have on it?

16. Some clocks have a hand that moves fast. When that hand goes all the way around the clock, how much time has passed?

17. The hand that moves fast went around 3 times. How much time passed?

18. In what country are peacocks wild animals?

19. A mile is a little more than ▇▇▇▇ feet.

A

1	2	3	4
1. terrible	1. jewels	1. <u>post</u>er	1. project
2. attack	2. earned	2. <u>hallelujah</u>	2. bought
3. behave	3. handful	3. <u>power</u>ful	3. reply
4. scar	4. prettier	4. <u>correct</u>	4. truth
5. scarred	5. returned	5. <u>plenty</u>	5. single
6. perhaps		6. <u>gentlemen</u>	6. homonym

B

The Big Fight

It was noon when three workers led Toby and his father from the cage to a small tent. There were about twenty people inside the tent waiting for the boxing kangaroos to put on their show.

One of the workers put boxing gloves on both kangaroos. Then the owner of the zoo stood between the two kangaroos and said, "Ladies and gentlemen— boxing kangaroos. You will see them box like champions. You will see them fight until one of them knocks the other out. They will use their gloves, but these powerful animals will also use their tails."

The owner of the zoo was right about some of the things he said but not all of them. The crowd did see the kangaroos use their gloves. The crowd also saw them use

their tails. But the two kangaroos did not hit each other. They had a plan. Toby's father winked at Toby. That was the signal for the two kangaroos to swing their little front legs as hard as they could. They both hit the owner of the zoo. Then the kangaroos swung their tails as hard as they could. Both tails hit the owner at the same time, and he went flying through the air.

Quickly Toby ran over to the people in the crowd. "Please, listen to me," he said, but they were not listening. They were clapping and cheering.

One person said, "This is the best act we ever saw. What boxing kangaroos."

"Please listen," Toby said. "We were taken from Australia by crooks . . . "

The people were still laughing and clapping. "What an act," they were shouting.

Suddenly, there was a terrible screech. The crowd became quiet. Then a very loud voice said, "The kangaroo is telling you the truth."

Toby said, "Good for Pip."

Pip was in his cage, but he had such a loud voice that the people could easily hear what he was saying. "I was taken from my home in India. For me, this was terrible. For you, of course, it is very nice because you get to look at me. But the people who brought us here are crooks. Somebody should call the police."

Somebody did call the police. By the time the police came to the zoo, four people were sitting on the owner so that he did not escape. The people had let out all the animals. One platypus kept shouting, "Hallelujah!" A small bear was eating a handful of peanuts. Toby and his father were standing next to Pip. And Pip was entertaining the people.

"Here's one that will amaze you," Pip said and turned around with his tail feathers shining. "Notice how the sunlight catches the feathers and makes them shine like jewels."

When the police started to take the owner away, the owner said, "You can't blame me for this. I bought these animals from Mabel."

"That's correct," Pip said. "Mabel is a crook."

The owner said, "I'll tell you where you can find Mabel and the captain." And he did.

•   •   •

Mabel is in jail. So are the captain and the three sailors.

Pip is still in Canada. When he thought about going back to India, he realized that there were many peacocks there, and some of them were even prettier than he was. So he decided that he would continue to entertain the people of Canada. He has a nice place in a real zoo. He has plenty of room to turn around and to show off.

The platypus went back to Australia. All the way back he kept saying, "Hallelujah!" The police took the bears, the snakes, and the apes to their homes.

That took care of just about everybody except Toby and his father. They went back to Australia too, where they found their mob.

When the other kangaroos saw Toby and his father, they cheered. "Toby saved us from hunters," they shouted. "Hooray for Toby!"

The leader said, "We are glad that two very important kangaroos have returned to our mob. Both these kangaroos have earned our thanks."

Now, when the mob moves from place to place, the leader hops first. Right behind him is a kangaroo with a very long tail that has three white spots on it. And right next to that kangaroo is a kangaroo that used to be called a joey. And right next to that kangaroo is Toby's mother.

And when the mob moves along, you may be able to hear one of the kangaroos saying, "Oh, good, good, good."

THE END

C Number your paper from 1 through 21.

Skill Items

Here are three events that happened in the story.
Write **beginning, middle,** or **end** for each event.

1. Toby and his father were taken to a small tent.

2. The police arrived.

3. The other kangaroos cheered when they saw Toby and his father.

Use the words in the box to write complete sentences.

sailors	perfectly	amount	colorful
correct	champions	surprise	loudly

4. She paid the ▮▮▮ ▮▮▮.

5. The ▮▮▮ performed ▮▮▮.

Review Items

6. Which letter shows a kangaroo?
7. Which letter shows a koala?
8. Which letter shows a platypus?

9. If you go east from Australia, what ocean do you go through?

10. If you go west from the United States, what ocean do you go through?

11. In what country are peacocks wild animals?

12. What is a group of kangaroos called?

13. What is a baby kangaroo called?

14. What's the name of the large, beautiful bird of India with a colorful tail?

15. How many meters long is that bird from its head to the end of its tail?

16. Which letter shows the stern?

17. Which letter shows the hold?

18. Which letter shows a deck?

19. Which letter shows the bow?

20. Which letter shows a bulkhead?

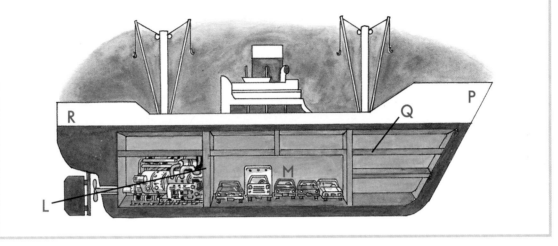

21. Write the letters of the 9 places that are in the United States.

a. Denver

b. Turkey

c. Chicago

d. China

e. Alaska

f. Italy

g. Lake Michigan

h. Japan

i. New York City

j. Texas

k. San Francisco

l. Ohio

m. California

n. Greece

o. Canada

p. Australia

SPECIAL PROJECT

Make a large poster that shows some of the animals that live in Australia. You may find pictures of animals of Australia in an encyclopedia or in other books. Your teacher will help you find some good pictures.

Make copies of the pictures you find. Put the pictures on a large poster. At the top of the poster write the title of the poster. Write the name of each animal near the picture of that animal. Below each animal write some facts about that animal.

◆ Tell what it eats.
◆ Tell what color it is.
◆ Tell how big it is.

A

1	2	3
1. involve	1. involved	1. batter
2. perhaps	2. scar	2. homonym
3. among	3. single	3. battered
4. constantly	4. scarred	4. behave
	5. terrible	5. attack
		6. reply

B

Homonyms

You're going to read a story about words that sometimes confuse people. These words are called **homonyms.** A homonym sounds the same as some other word. But a homonym is spelled differently. Remember, two homonyms sound the same, but their spelling is different.

Here are two homonyms: **four** and **for.**

Here are two other homonyms: **new** and **knew.**

The word **eight** has a homonym. Other numbers have homonyms.

The sentence below has four words that are homonyms: **She rode for one hour.**

The first homonym is the word **rode.**

What's the next homonym?

What's the next homonym?

What's the last homonym?

You'll read more about those homonyms.

Remember the name we use for words that sound the same as other words.

C   The Scarred Words in the Word Bank

If you look at the words in the word bank, you'll notice that some of them have scars. These scars came from great fights that used to take place right in the word bank. The words no longer fight, but thousands of years ago when Hohoboho was a very young country, there were hundreds of terrible fights. Words would leap out of their seats and attack other words. They would hit and fight and scratch and yell and throw things and behave like a bunch of animals. From these fights some words got their scars.

Not all the words have scars. The word **wash** does not have one single scar. Neither does the word **only** or the word **run.** But the word **red** has scars. The word **their** is covered with scars. So is the word **two.**

Here's the story about why some words are scarred: When the word bank opened for the first time, the words were given their seats. The people in Hohoboho would talk, and every time one of the words was said, that word would get one point. ⭐ But there was a very bad problem. Some words sounded just like other words. When somebody in Hohoboho said, "It is over **there,**" the word **there** would say, "That's me. I get that point." The word **their** would say, "No, that's me. The person said **their.**"

By now both words would be standing up and hollering at each other. And then the words would start swinging and scratching and throwing things.

The fight would continue until the words were tired out. By then somebody in Hohoboho would say something like, "Do they have a radio in **their** car?"

The word **their** would jump up, "That's me."

"No way," the word **there** would reply. "Somebody said **there** and that's me."

Soon, the two words would be fighting again.

As **their** and **there** fought, somebody in Hohoboho would say, "Speak louder. I can't **hear** you." The word **hear** would jump up and say, "That's me." The word **here** would jump up and say, "That's me." Then **here** and **hear** would get into a terrible fight.

In other parts of the word bank, other words would be shouting and fighting.

MORE NEXT TIME

D **Number your paper from 1 through 12.**

Review Items

1. Write the letters of all the words that belong to the **jump** family.

2. Write the letters of all the words that belong to the **ride** family.

a. ride	e. rode	i. jumps	m. hiding	q. riding
b. jumping	f. rider	j. rides	n. see	r. eats
c. hot	g. sitting	k. chair	o. jumped	s. jump
d. book	h. talked	l. jumper	p. flying	t. run

Some of Andrew's hang-times are shown on the stopwatches.

3. Write the letter of the watch that shows his best hang-time.

4. How many seconds are shown on that watch?

5. Write the letter of the watch that shows his worst hang-time.

6. How many seconds are shown on that watch?

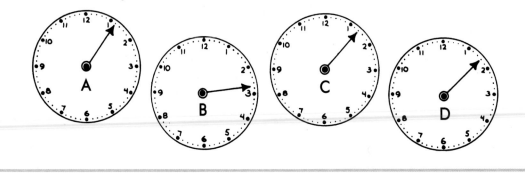

7. Write the letters of 3 ways that people traveled 2 hundred years ago.

    a. by water   b. by jet   c. by train

    d. by walking   e. by car   f. by horse

8. Is the United States **bigger** than most other countries or **smaller** than most other countries?

9. Which country is smaller, the United States or Canada?

10. What place does the **A** show?

11. What place does the **B** show?

12. What place does the **C** show?

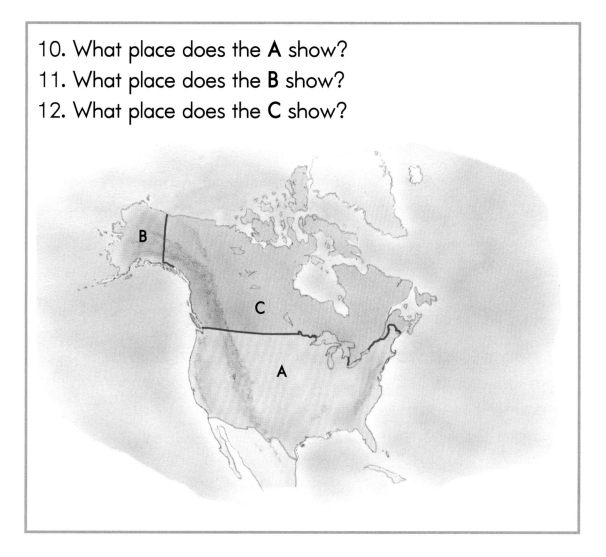

A

1	2
1. calm	1. plugs
2. describe	2. earplugs
3. among	3. involved
4. eight	4. constantly
	5. battered

B # Henry Ouch Takes a Vacation

Henry Ouch went for a vacation. He left San Francisco on a large ship. That ship went to Japan. You know which direction it went.

How far was that trip?

What ocean did Henry cross?

The ship passed some islands. How did Henry know they were islands? Henry could see palm trees on some islands. He knew the name for branches of a palm tree. He also knew the name of the large hard things that grow on some palm trees. When Henry got thirsty, he drank little drops of water that formed on the deck early in the morning. What are those drops called?

Henry did not drink water from the ocean. Why not?

Henry did not like it when the temperature dropped down because Henry's body worked like the bodies of other insects. Henry was ▮▮▮▮-blooded. Sometimes the temperature inside his body was higher than your normal temperature.

Sometimes the temperature inside his body was lower than your normal temperature.

C   The Number with the Most Scars

❀ The words in the word bank had a problem because they listened to the words that were said by the people in Hohoboho. Some words sound the same. When the people in Hohoboho said these words, the words that sounded the same would fight over who got the point. The words **their** and **there** were always fighting. But they were not the only ones. The words for numbers were involved in some of the worst fights you could imagine. The word **three** never fought. Nor did the words **five, six,** or **seven.** But **one, two, four,** and **eight** went from ❀ one fight to another.

The word **one** fought with the word **won.** Every time somebody in Hohoboho said, "I **won,**" a fight would take place. Every time somebody in Hohoboho said, "You have **one** more turn," another fight would take place.

The word **four** was always fighting with **for.** If somebody in Hohoboho said, "I will do something **for** you," the words **for** and **four** would fight. They also fought when somebody said, "I have **four** spoons."

The word **eight** was always fighting with the word **ate.** If somebody said, "A man **ate** an egg," there would be a fight. The word **eight** would say, "Somebody said **eight.** That's me." The word **ate** would say, "You're crazy. Somebody said **ate.**" And the fight would start.

Eight, four, and **one** had terrible fights and lots of them, but their fights could not compare to the fights that the word **two** used to have. If you look at **two** now, you can get some idea of how bad those fights were. **Two** has scars and scars and scars. The reason is that **two** used to fight constantly. **Two** used to fight with the word **to.** Every time somebody would say, "Go **to** the store," **two** would say, "That's me. She said **two.**" Soon, **two** and **to** would be fighting.

But **two** also had fights with **too.** If somebody said, "I'll go, **too,**" **two** would say, "Another point for me. She said **two.**"

"No," **too** would say. "She said **too.**"

By now the word **to** would say, "You're both crazy," and a big fight would start.

By the end of the day, when the people in Hohoboho stopped talking and went to bed, some of the words in the word bank were pretty battered up. The word **two** was always among the words that were the most battered. **Two** was usually glad when the day was over. **Two** needed the rest before starting another day of battles with **too** and **to.**

MORE NEXT TIME

D Number your paper from 1 through 16.

Skill Items

> **Perhaps they will reply in a few days.**
> 1. What word means **maybe**?
> 2. What word means **answer**?

Review Items

3. A word that sounds the same as another word is called a ▮▮▮▮.

4. Find **S** on map 1. What place does the **S** show?
5. What's the name of place **R?**
6. Find **F** on map 2. What place does the **F** show?
7. What happened in place **F** about 3 thousand years ago?
8. What's the name of place **G?**
9. What's the name of place **H?**
10. What place does the **T** show?

Map 1   Map 2

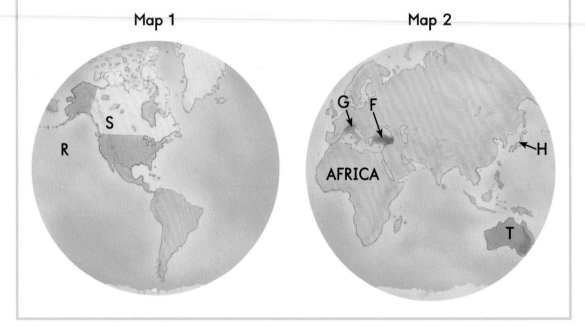

Copy words 11 through 16. After each word, write the letter of the word it fought with.

11. right
12. there
13. knew
14. road
15. do
16. ate

a. dew
b. write
c. eight
d. new
e. their
f. rode

A

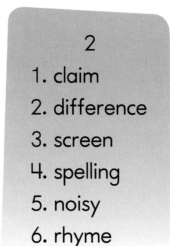

1

1. guard
2. language
3. describe
4. calm
5. earplugs
6. apostrophe

2

1. claim
2. difference
3. screen
4. spelling
5. noisy
6. rhyme

B

A Pilot's Trip

A jet pilot went around the world. She went from the country of Japan. She flew over China and Turkey and she landed in Italy. In what direction was she going?

Then she continued in the same direction until she came to a country that is much larger than Japan or Italy. She landed her jet plane in a city on the east coast of the country.

The pilot was not feeling well. She thought she had a slight fever. So she went to a doctor. The doctor told her that her temperature was normal. The doctor said, "You need more exercise. You should walk more than 5 thousand feet every day." The pilot knew the name of a unit that is a little more than 5 thousand feet.

The pilot took off and flew to a country where kangaroos live. There she saw a large group of kangaroos. She had a nice vacation.

C Some Words Stop Fighting

The word bank was a mess. That's the best way to describe it. Early in the morning, before the people in Hohoboho started to talk, things in the word bank would be calm. But before long a fight would start. Somebody in Hohoboho would say, "I have **new** shoes," and the fight would start between **new** and **knew.**

Then the people in Hohoboho would start talking more and more and more. And fights would start all over the word bank. It would become so noisy that some of the words wore earplugs. When a word wore earplugs it could not hear if it was said, but the words in the back of the bank didn't care.

The word **billows** almost always wore earplugs. The word **usually** sat near **billows.** Once **usually** pulled an earplug from **billows'** ear and asked, "Why do you wear earplugs? Don't you want to hear your name said?"

"Sure," **billows** replied. "But I'm not going to be said more than once or twice a day, and I'd rather have it quiet than listen to all this fighting and shouting."

After a while, things got so bad in the word bank that a change was made. If that change hadn't been made, some of the words might have been battered to pieces in the terrible fights they had. But one morning there was an announcement. A voice came over the loudspeaker and said, "From now on, the words will appear on the screen when ★ the people of Hohoboho say them. You will not hear what the people say. But you will see how the words are spelled. If you are spelled the same way as a word on the screen, you get a point."

The words looked at each other. The word **their** looked at **there.** The word **their** said, "I think that will work. My spelling is different from your spelling. If they write the words, we will be able to tell if the word is **their** or **there.**"

And that's just what happened. When the words were said by the people in Hohoboho, the words would appear on a large screen. And that was the very last fight that **two** had or that **there** had or that **eight** had. The word **one** shook hands with the word **won.** "This is great," the word **one** said. The word **hear** and the word **here** also shook hands.

There wasn't any word happier about this change than the word **two.** For the first time since the word bank opened, the word **two** could jump up and say, "That's me. They said **two,**" without getting into a fight with **to** and **too.**

The change in the word bank stopped the fights among words that sound the same. But there was a new problem. As soon as the words appeared on the screen, fights started among words that had never fought before. Can you think of why these fights would take place?

MORE NEXT TIME

D Number your paper from 1 through 18.

Skill Items

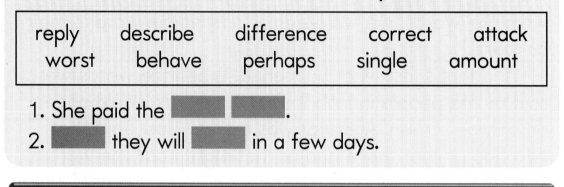

Use the words in the box to write complete sentences.

reply	describe	difference	correct	attack
worst	behave	perhaps	single	amount

1. She paid the ▮▮ ▮▮.
2. ▮▮ they will ▮▮ in a few days.

Review Items

3. Did the first people who lived in caves cook their food?

4. Did the people who lived in caves many years later cook their food?

5. What's the name of the large, beautiful bird of India with a colorful tail?

6. How long is that bird from its head to the end of its tail?

7. What do we call the part of a ship where the cargo is carried?

8. Name the country that is just north of the United States.

9. How many seconds are in one minute?

10. Which letter shows where Australia is?

11. Which letter shows where the United States is?

12. Which letter shows where Canada is?

13. Which letter shows where the Pacific Ocean is?

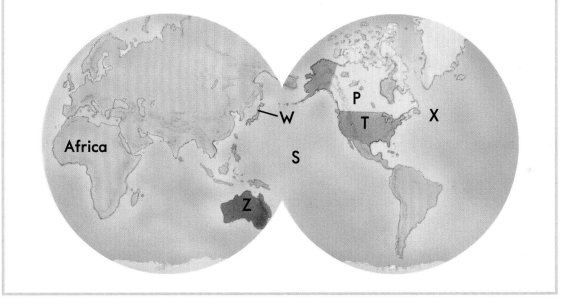

Copy words 14 through 18. After each word, write the letter of the word it fought with.

14. for   a. hear

15. too   b. one

16. won   c. two

17. here   d. four

18. knew   e. new

A

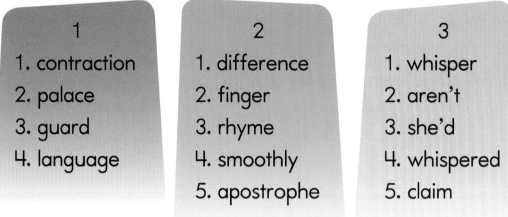

1	2	3
1. contraction	1. difference	1. whisper
2. palace	2. finger	2. aren't
3. guard	3. rhyme	3. she'd
4. language	4. smoothly	4. whispered
	5. apostrophe	5. claim

B ## Another Change Is Made

New fights started in the word bank as soon as the words were written on the screen. To understand the problem that took place in the word bank, you have to understand that some words are spelled the same way but are not said the same way. They sound different.

Two words are spelled with the letters **r-o-w.** One of those words rhymes with **now.** Say that word. The other word that is spelled **r-o-w** rhymes with **go.** Say that word.

The two words that are spelled **r-o-w** never fought until the words were written on the screen. But as soon as the words appeared on the screen, these words fought.

When somebody in Hohoboho would say, "Let's plant these seeds in a **row,**" the two words spelled **r-o-w** would jump up. "That's me," they would start yelling. Soon they would be fighting.

Two other words that are spelled the same are spelled **w-i-n-d.** One of those words rhymes with **find.** The other word rhymes with **pinned.** But every time the word spelled **w-i-n-d** appeared on the screen, these two words started to fight over who got the point.

Some terrible fights took place over the word spelled **r-e-a-d.** Somebody in Hohoboho would say, "Did you **read** that?" The other person would answer, "Yes, I **read** that." Both words spelled **r-e-a-d** would get into a terrible row.

Another pair of words that had some bad fights are spelled **t-e-a-r.** Somebody in Hohoboho would say, "I think you're crying. Is that a **tear** in your eye?" And both words would try to claim the point. "That's me," they would shout. The same words would fight when somebody said, "Take that paper and **tear** it up."

If you looked at the words that were involved in these fights, you'd see that they have some small scars, but not many scars and not very ⭐ bad ones. Compared to the word **two,** the words spelled **t-e-a-r** would look as if they had never been in a fight. Here's the reason that the words with the same spelling are not very scarred: A few days after the fights started another announcement was made. The voice said, "From now on, the words will go on the screen. Then a voice will read the words. Here's how a word in the word bank gets a point. That word must be spelled the same as the word on the screen. The word must also sound the same as the word the voice reads."

The word **slow** said, "I don't understand that rule."

The word **smart** said, "It's easy. If you're spelled like the word on the screen and if you sound like that word, you get a point."

The word **confusion** said, "It sounds too hard."

The word **clear** said, "Look at it this way. If you get mixed up, I'll tell you if you get the point."

Lazy said, "That sounds good to me."

Then the words with problems began to talk.

One of the words spelled **t-e-a-r** said, "That makes sense. If somebody says my name, we will hear it. We don't have to fight."

The words spelled **r-e-a-d** agreed. "You can hear the difference when somebody says, 'I will **read** a book' or says 'Yesterday, I **read** a book.'"

So there was a big change in the word bank. The words that sound the same didn't fight because they could look at the screen to see how the word was spelled. The word **two** didn't fight with the words that sounded the same. And the words that are spelled the same never had a problem because they listened to the voice. If the voice said, "That is a **live** fish," the sound of the word would tell who got the point. Most of the problems in the word bank were solved.

MORE NEXT TIME

C **Number your paper from 1 through 18.**

Skill Items

Write the word from the box that means the same thing as the underlined part of each sentence.

continued	couple	thawed	boiling
announcement	argument	enormous	comparison

1. The snow <u>melted</u> when the sun came out.
2. The storm clouds were <u>very large</u>.
3. The teacher's <u>message</u> told about our homework.

Review Items

4. The names in one box tell about time. Write the letter of that box.

5. The names in one box tell about length. Write the letter of that box.

A	centimeter inch meter mile yard
B	week year second month minute hour

6. How fast is truck **A** going?
7. How fast is truck **B** going?
8. Which truck is going faster?

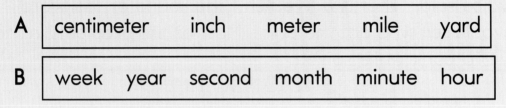

A   20   B   40

9. Write the letter of the animal that is facing into the wind.

10. Which direction is that animal facing?

11. So what's the **name** of that wind?

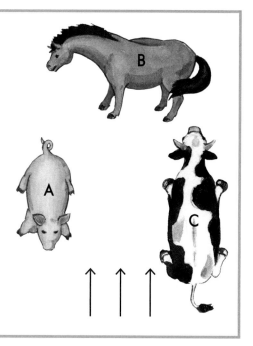

12. Which country is warmer, Canada or the United States?

13. Where do more people live, in Canada or in the United States?

Write a homonym for each word.

14. rode

15. write

16. eight

17. new

18. one

A

1	2	3
1. future	1. <u>pa</u>lace	1. smooth and quiet
2. possible	2. <u>near</u>by	2. contractions
3. guards	3. <u>she</u>'d	3. yesterday
4. travel	4. <u>are</u>n't	4. apostrophe
5. traveler	5. <u>whis</u>per	5. languages
6. brick		

B   CONTRACTIONS

Contractions are words made by joining two words together. Part of one word is missing. This mark ' is called an **apostrophe.** It is used to show where part of the word is missing.

Here are some contractions and the words that make them up:

- **Couldn't** is made up of **could** and **not.**
- **He'll** is made up of **he** and **will.**
- **You've** is made up of **you** and **have.**

Say the words that make up each contraction below.

a. **We've** is made up of ▬▬ and ▬▬.

b. **You're** is made up of ▬▬ and ▬▬.

c. **Can't** is made up of ▬▬ and ▬▬.

d. **I'll** is made up of ▬▬ and ▬▬.

C The Last Problem in the Word Bank Is Solved

Perhaps you think that all the problems in the word bank had been solved. The words that sound the same as other words were no longer fighting. The words that are spelled the same as other words were friends again. Almost everything was going smoothly. There was still one problem, however. Words that are contractions had fights. Here are some contractions: **you're, I'll, can't, couldn't, shouldn't, aren't, she'd.** Can you name some other contractions?

The contractions fought because contractions are made up of two words. The contraction **couldn't** is made up of the words **could** and **not.**

The contraction **you're** is made up of the words **you** and **are.** The contraction **I'll** is made of two other words. What words make up the contraction **shouldn't?**

Here's what used to happen in the word bank. Whenever a contraction was named, the two words that make up the contraction would fight. For example, when the contraction **you'll** was said, the word **you** would say, "That's me." The word **will** would say, "No, that's me." A third word would join the fight. That word was the contraction **you'll.** So a big row would go on between **you'll, you,** and **will.**

Which three words would fight when someone in Hohoboho said, **she'll?** Which three words would fight when someone said **shouldn't?**

By now, the other words in the word bank were tired of seeing words fight. "Come on," the word **calm** said. "Why don't you  figure out some way of solving the problem? Do you have to wait for another announcement?"

"Yeah," the word **smart** said. "We can work out a plan that will make everybody happy."

The word **question** asked, "What kind of plan would that be?"

So the word **smart** thought for a moment and then came up with this plan: every time a contraction is said, three words get points. The contraction that is said gets one point. The word in the contraction that has all its letters gets one point. The word in the contraction that has some letters missing does not get one point. That word gets half a point. **Smart** said, "Remember, the contraction and the full word each get one point."

The contraction **shouldn't** said, "I think I understand. If somebody says **shouldn't,** I get one point. And **should** gets one point because it has all its letters."

The word **not** said, "And I only get half a point because one of my letters is missing in the word **shouldn't.**"

The plan worked, and the fighting finally ended in the word bank. When a word like **you'll** is said, the contraction **you'll** gets one point. The word **you** gets one point because it has no part missing. The word **will** gets half a point because it has a part missing.

"Things are very nice in the word bank now," the word **calm** said when the plan was first used.

"Yes, things are nice," the word **quiet** whispered.

THE END

D Number your paper from 1 through 15.

Here's a rule: **Insects do not have bones.**

1. A beetle is an insect. So what else do you know about a beetle?

2. A worm is not an insect. So what else do you know about a worm?

3. An ant is an insect. So what else do you know about an ant?

Review Items

4. If you go east from Australia, what ocean do you go through?

5. A kangaroo is ▮▮▮▮ centimeters long when it is born.

6. Big kangaroos grow to be as big as a ▮▮▮▮.

7. A kangaroo that sits on a hill and warns the mob when trouble is coming is called a ▮▮▮▮.

8. What does a male peacock spread when it shows off?

9. Which is more beautiful, a peacock's feathers or a peacock's voice?

10. Which letter shows the stern?

11. Which letter shows the hold?

12. Which letter shows a deck?

13. Which letter shows the bow?

14. Which letter shows a bulkhead?

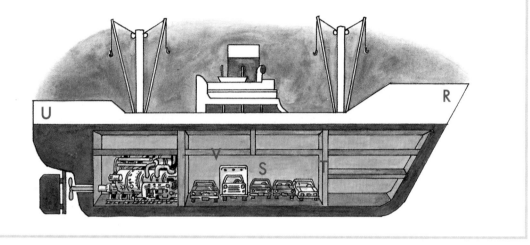

15. Boxers wear large mittens when they box. What are those mittens called?

A

1	2	3
1. bicycle	1. heart	1. future
2. fruit	2. nearby	2. Chicago
3. wooden	3. spread	3. possible
4. brick	4. reasons	4. travelers
	5. greater	5. yesterday

B

Wooden Buildings

In large cities, houses may be made of wood, but most of the other buildings are not made of wood. There are a lot of reasons that office buildings and stores are not made of wood. Buildings made of steel, concrete, and brick are stronger than buildings made of wood. Some office buildings are very tall, but it would not be possible to make such tall buildings out of wood.

Another reason that stores and office buildings are not made of wood is that wooden buildings may burn. The buildings in a city are close together, so when a building catches on fire, the fire may spread to buildings that are nearby. In a city with many wooden buildings, a fire could burn down the whole city. That is what happened in Chicago in the year 1871. The buildings were made of wood and a fire spread through the whole city.

Chicago is not the only city that had a great fire that spread through wooden buildings. You will soon read about another one of those cities.

C Time Machines

In the next lesson, you'll read about a time machine. There are no real time machines, but there are stories about them. In these stories, the time machine takes people into the future or the past. You could go back to the year men first landed on the moon. Or you could go to the year 2050. When time travelers go into the past, they see how things were years ago. When they go into the future, they see how things will be years from now.

In the story you will read, the people in the time machine feel a great force as they go through time. A force is a push. The greater the force, the harder the push. If you put a book on top of your hand, your hand will feel the force of that book pushing down on your hand. If you pile ten books on your hand, your hand will feel much more force. If you were in the time machine that you will read about, you might feel the force of 500 books pushing against parts of your body.

D More About a Time Line

You're going to read about some things that took place a long time ago and other things that will take place in the future.

The future is the time that has not happened yet. Tomorrow is part of the future. Next week is part of the future. Yesterday is not part of the future. It is part of the past.

What year is it now?

A year with a larger number is in the future. A year with a smaller number is in the past. The year 2300 is about 300 years in the future. The year 1700 is about 300 years in the past.

Let's say a girl was living in the year 2005. For her, the year 2004 would be in the past. For her, the year 2006 would be in the future.

Remember the rule about time: **The numbers for the years get smaller as you go back in the past.**

Look at time line 1. This is like a time line you have seen. The word **now** is 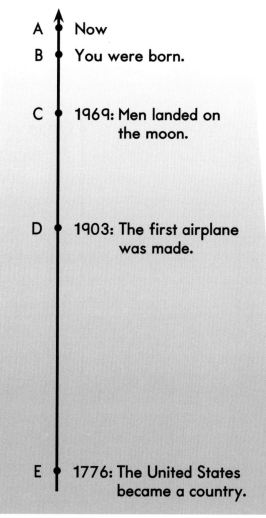 at the top of this time line.

Touch dot A. That's the year for now. What is it?

Touch dot B. That dot shows when you were born. What year goes at dot B?

Touch dot C. That dot shows when men landed on the moon. What year was that?

Touch dot D. That dot shows when the first airplane was made. What year was that?

Touch dot E. That dot shows the year the United States became a country. What year was that?

A — Now

B — You were born.

C — 1969: Men landed on the moon.

D — 1903: The first airplane was made.

E — 1776: The United States became a country.

TIME LINE 1

Time line 2 shows the future. The future is the part above **now.** On the time line, dot F is the year 2020.

What year is dot G?

Which is farther in the future, the year 2020 or the year 2320?

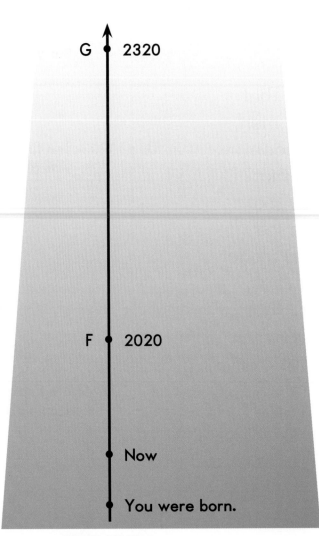

TIME LINE 2

E Number your paper from 1 through 28.

1. If all buildings in a city are made of wood, what could happen?

2. In a large city, some buildings may be made of wood. What kind of buildings are those?
   - office buildings • stores • houses • barns

3. In a large city, some buildings are not made of wood. What kind of buildings are those?
   - office buildings • stores • houses • barns

4. Which city had a great fire that burned down most of the city?

5. In what year was that fire?

6. Taller buildings are made of steel, concrete, and brick because they are ▮▮▮.
   - taller • stronger • cheaper

Passage C

7. Are time machines **real** or **make-believe?**

8. A force is a ▮▮▮.

9. Which picture shows the largest force?
10. Which picture shows the smallest force?

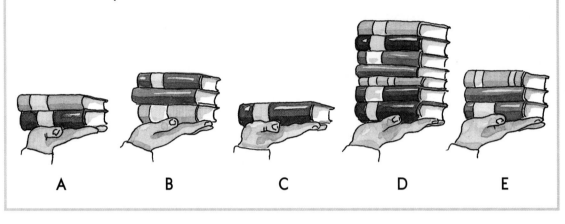

A   B   C   D   E

Skill Items

Write the word from the box that means the same thing as the underlined part of each sentence.

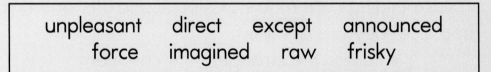

| unpleasant | direct | except | announced |
| force | imagined | raw | frisky |

11. The path between their houses was <u>straight</u>.

12. The hot weather was <u>not very nice</u>.

13. Susan ate <u>uncooked</u> fish.

Review Items

14. The temperature inside your body is about 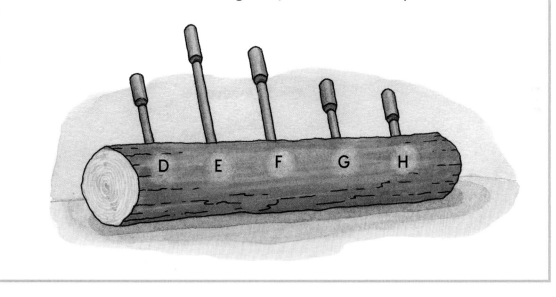 degrees when you are healthy.

15. Most fevers don't go over ▬▬▬▬ degrees.

16. Airplanes land at airports. Ships land at ▬▬▬▬.

17. Airplanes are pulled by little trucks. Ships are pulled by ▬▬▬▬.

18. Airplanes unload at gates. Ships unload at ▬▬▬▬.

---

19. You would have the least amount of power if you pushed against one of the handles. Which handle is that?

20. Which handle would give you the most power?

21. Which is longer, a centimeter or a meter?

22. How many centimeters long is a meter?

23. An arrow goes from the **R.** Which direction is that arrow going?

24. An arrow goes from the **S.** Which direction is that arrow going?

25. An arrow goes from the **T.** Which direction is that arrow going?

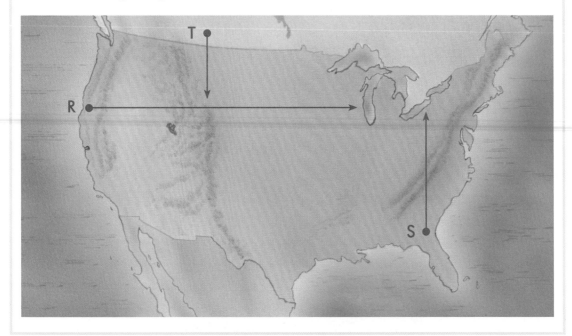

26. How many ships sailed to Troy?

27 How long did the war between Greece and Troy go on?

28. If the Greek army could get a few men inside the wall of Troy, these men could ███████.

A

1	2
1. argument	1. Thrig
2. convince	2. metal
3. appliance	3. heart
4. clicked	4. fruit
5. dials	5. Eric
6. flashing	6. bicycles

B

Eric and Tom
Find a Time Machine

Eric and Tom were with some other boys and girls. They had been at a picnic that was halfway up the mountain. Now they were walking home with the other boys and girls. As they walked down the mountain, they could see the town off in the distance.

Eric was tired. "Tom," he said, "let's rest."

Tom said, "I don't think that's a good idea. It's going to get dark pretty soon, and we might get lost."

"That's silly," Eric said. "All we have to do is follow the path. It goes right back to town. Are you scared?"

Tom said, "I'm not scared of anything."

It was very quiet up there on the side of the mountain—very quiet. The lights in the town were coming on. The other kids were far away by now. A cool breeze was blowing down the side of the mountain.

Then suddenly there was a loud sound. "Crrrrsssssk."

Tom jumped up. "Wh—what was that?"

Tom saw something flash through the sky.

It landed on the side of the mountain right above them. It looked like a metal pill. And it was as big as some of the trees on the mountain.

"Let's get out of here," Tom said. He grabbed Eric's arm, but Eric didn't move. He was standing there with his mouth open, looking at the pill.

Just then a door on the side of the thing opened, and an old man stepped out. He waved to Eric and Tom. "Hello," he called.

"Let's get out of here," Tom said again. Tom's heart was beating so hard that his shirt was shaking.

Eric waved to the old man. "Hello," Eric called and started running toward the metal pill.

"Come back," Tom called. But Eric ran up to the old man. The old man was sitting on the ground. He did not look well. He was wearing a strange metal coat.

"Who are you?" Eric asked.

The old man said, "My name is Thrig."

Eric said, "Where do you live?"

Thrig said, "I live on Earth. But I live in a different time than you."

Tom and Eric looked at each other. Tom thought, "How can somebody live in a different time?"

Thrig then told Eric and Tom a very strange story. Thrig told them that he lived in the year 2400.

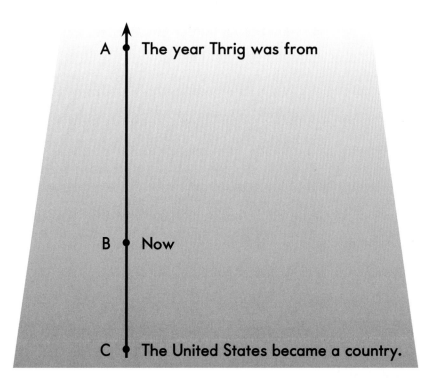

A • The year Thrig was from

B • Now

C • The United States became a country.

Tom said, "The year 2400 will not ⭐ be here for 4 hundred years. That year is 4 hundred years in the future."

Thrig nodded. "Yes, I live in the future," he said. He told the boys that he had made a time machine. This machine was the large metal pill. It could take him into the past or into the future. Thrig had just gone back in time 4 hundred years.

Thrig said, "But now I cannot go back to the year 2400. I am old. And when the machine goes through time, it puts a great force on a person's body. I do not think that I have enough strength to return to 2400." Thrig said, "I will spend the rest of my life here. I will never see my friends again."

Thrig looked very sad. "And now I must rest. The trip through time has made me very tired." Thrig closed his eyes.

"He's asleep," Eric said after a moment. Then Eric walked toward the time machine.

Tom grabbed his arm and said, "Let's get out of here before something happens."

Eric laughed. He said, "That time machine won't bite you." Eric pulled away and started toward the door of the giant machine.

Tom ran after Eric. He caught up just as Eric was going through the door.

The inside of the time machine was filled with dials and lights. There were red lights and green lights and orange lights. There were big dials and little dials. There were dials that buzzed and dials that clicked. "Let's get out of here," Tom said.

Eric walked over to a seat in the middle of the machine. He sat down. As soon as he sat down, the door closed. "Swwwwwwshshshsh."

🌸 Eric grabbed one of the handles. "I wonder what this handle does."

"Don't touch it," Tom said. "Don't touch it."

Eric pulled the handle down a little bit. Suddenly more lights started going on. Dials started moving and clicking and buzzing. And then Tom felt a great force. He could feel it push against his face and his chest.

"We—we're going through time," Tom announced.

He heard Eric's voice. It sounded very far away. "Oh, no," Eric cried.

And then everything was quiet. The dials slowed down. Most of the lights stopped flashing.

Eric stood up and the door 🌸 opened. The boys looked outside. For a long time they looked. They could not believe what they saw.

MORE NEXT TIME

C Number your paper from 1 through 22.

Skill Items

Here are 3 events that happened in the story. Write **beginning, middle,** or **end** for each event.
1. Tom felt a great force against his face and his chest.
2. Eric and Tom were walking down a mountain with some boys and girls.
3. A time machine landed on the side of the mountain.

The palace guards spoke different languages.
4. What's the name of the place where a king and queen live?
5. What word refers to the words that people in a country use to say things?
6. What word names the people who protect the palace?

Review Items

7. Which arrow shows the way the air will leave the jet engines?
8. Which arrow shows the way the jet will move?

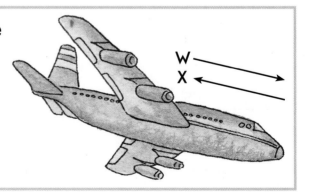

9. The biggest state in the United States is ▬▬▬.

10. The second biggest state in the United States is ▬▬▬.

11. Write the name of the state in the United States that is bigger than Japan.
    - Ohio
    - New York
    - Alaska

12. Write the letter of the plane that is in the warmest air.

13. Write the letter of the plane that is in the coldest air.

Z	5 miles high
Y	4 miles high
X	3 miles high
	2 miles high
W	1 mile high

14. A force is a ▬▬▬.

15. If all buildings in a city are made of wood, what could happen?

16. Taller buildings are made of steel and brick because they are ▬▬▬.
    - cheaper
    - taller
    - stronger

17. Which city had a great fire that burned down most of the city?

18. In what year was that fire?

19. Which picture shows the largest force?

20. Which picture shows the smallest force?

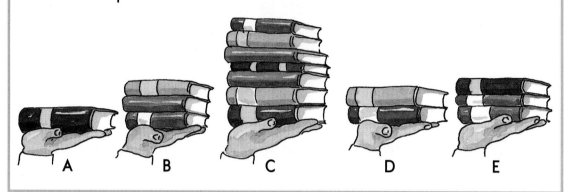

A   B   C   D   E

21. In a large city, some buildings are not made of wood. What kind of buildings are those?
    • office buildings   • stores   • houses   • barns

22. In a large city, some buildings may be made of wood. What kind of buildings are those?

Number your paper from 1 through 33.

1. Boxers wear large mittens when they box. What are those mittens called?

2. A word that sounds the same as another word is called a ▮▮▮▮.

3. Let's say that someone in Hohoboho said, "My friends got hurt in a **row.**" The word that would get the point rhymes with ▮▮▮▮.

   • how   • no

4. Let's say that someone in Hohoboho said, "Do you **live** near her?" The word that would get the point rhymes with ▮▮▮▮.

   • dive   • give

5. Let's say that someone in Hohoboho said, "I like to **read.**" The word that would get the point rhymes with ▮▮▮▮.

   • need   • bed

Write a homonym for each word.
   6. dew
   7. to
   8. hear
   9. new
  10. won
  11. road

For each contraction, write the two words that make up the contraction.

  12. you're   13. we'll   14. can't   15. I've

16. A force is a ▮▮▮. The greater the force, the harder the ▮▮▮.

17. Which picture shows the smallest force?
18. Which picture shows the largest force?

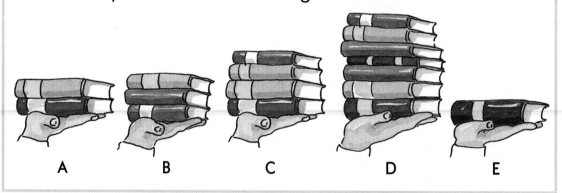

A   B   C   D   E

19. In what year did Eric and Tom find the time machine?

20. What year was Thrig from?
21. Is that year **in the past** or **in the future**?

22. What do you do to close the door of the time machine?

23. What do you do to make the time machine move in time?

24. If all buildings in a city are made of wood, what could happen?

25. In a large city, some buildings may be made of wood. What kind of buildings are those?
    - office buildings   - stores   - houses   - barns

26. In a large city, some buildings are not made of wood. What kind of buildings are those?

27. Which city had a great fire that burned down most of the city?

28. In what year was that fire?

29. Taller buildings are made of steel and brick because they are ▮▮▮.
    - taller   - stronger   - cheaper

Skill Items

For each item, write the underlined word from the sentences in the box.

> She paid the <u>correct</u> <u>amount</u>.
> <u>Perhaps</u> they will <u>reply</u> in a few days.

30. What underlining means **answer?**
31. What underlining means **right?**
32. What underlining means **maybe?**
33. What underlining tells **how much there is?**

END OF TEST 13

A

1	2	3	4
1. buried	1. <u>earth</u>quake	1. clomping	1. we'd
2. Egypt	2. <u>street</u>light	2. wider	2. center
3. pyramid	3. <u>news</u>paper	3. waking	3. hay
4. pocket	4. <u>tug</u>boat	4. bicycles	4. lean
5. slave		5. words	5. April
6. argument		6. convinced	6. fruit

B More About Time

In today's story, you'll find out what year Tom and Eric went to in the time machine.

That year was in the past, not in the future.

So you know that they did not go to some of the years below. Tell which years they did not go to.

a. 2450   b. 1880   c. 1900   d. 2600

Touch dot B on the time line. That is the year that Eric and Tom found the time machine. What year is that?

Touch dot A on the time line. That is the year that Thrig was from. What year is that?

Is that year in the past or in the future?

About how many years in the future?

Touch dot C. That is the year Tom and Eric went to. It is very close to the year the first airplane was made. What year was the first airplane made?

Did Tom and Eric go to a time that was **before** or **after** the first airplane?

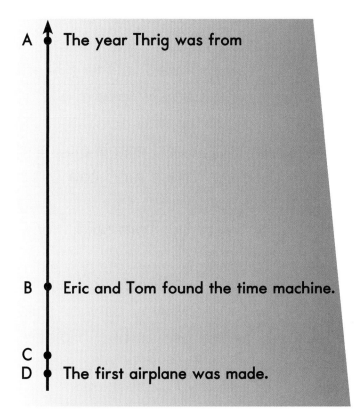

A — The year Thrig was from

B — Eric and Tom found the time machine.

C

D — The first airplane was made.

C The San Francisco Earthquake

Tom and Eric looked out of the time machine. They were on the side of a mountain. Tom could see a large city in the distance. Lights were on all over the city, but they did not look very bright.

"Let's go down there," Eric said.

Tom said, "Remember, we don't know where we are. Let's be careful."

By the time the boys got to the city, the sky was very dark. The city had buildings and streets, but there was something strange about the city.

"I know what's funny," Tom said. "Most of the streets are made of dirt." Tom pointed to the streetlights. "Those are gas streetlights," he said. "Those are the kind of streetlights they had a long time ago."

Just then a clomping sound came down the street. The boys hid behind a fence. The sound came from a wagon that was pulled by a horse.

After the wagon went by, Tom said, "We've gone back in time, all right."

Eric said, "Things don't look very different."

Tom said, "You don't see any cars or trucks, do you?"

Then Tom said, "We'd better find a place to sleep."

They found a barn outside the city. They slept in the hay. Tom did not sleep very well. He had bad dreams.

Very early in the morning, the boys started to walk toward the center of the city. On the way they saw a newspaper in the street. They looked at the first page of the newspaper. The words that were at the top of the page said, "San Francisco Times."

Eric asked, "What's San Francisco?"

"San Francisco is a city," Tom said. "It is near the Pacific

Ocean." Tom looked at the date at the top of the newspaper: April 18, 1906.

Tom felt dizzy. He said, "We've  gone back in time about a hundred years." Just then Tom remembered that something happened in San Francisco in 1906, but he couldn't remember what.

Tom looked up. Three boys were standing in the street. They were wearing funny pants that stopped just below their knees. They were laughing at Tom and Eric. The tallest boy said to Tom, "You sure have funny clothes."

Tom looked at the clothes he and Eric were wearing. They didn't look funny to him.

"Let's get out of here," Eric said. "Let's go downtown."

The boys walked past blocks and blocks of buildings. Some of the buildings were little and some were pretty big. But most of them were made of wood.

Most people were riding horses or they were riding in wagons pulled by horses. Some boys and girls rode bicycles. Tom and Eric saw only one car. It was one of the very first cars ever made. When the car went by, a horse went wild and started to run down the street. The horse was pulling a wagon full of fruit. Fruit spilled all over the street. Tom and Eric picked up some apples.

Just then, the street shook. The ground moved to one side. It moved so fast that Eric fell down. Then the ground moved the other way, and Tom could see a large crack starting to form right in the middle of the street.

Tom yelled, "I remember what happened in 1906. The earthquake! The San Francisco earthquake!"

Tom could hardly hear his own voice. People were screaming and running from buildings. A building on the corner started to lean and then it fell into the street. The crack in the middle of the street suddenly got wider and longer. The crack ran down the street. A horse and wagon slid and fell into the crack.

Suddenly, fires started to break out all along the crack. The crack had broken the gas lines, and now the gas was burning. Buildings were burning. The ground was shaking. People were running and screaming. Buildings were falling. "We've got to get out of here," Tom yelled.

Hundreds of men and women pushed this way and that way. The ground shook again. Another great crack formed in the street. It ran across the street and ran right between Eric and Tom. The crack got wider and wider. And suddenly Eric fell into the crack.

MORE NEXT TIME

D Number your paper from 1 through 21.

Skill Items

Use the words in the box to write complete sentences.

guards	amazing	languages	stretched
palace	future	reply	flashed	perhaps

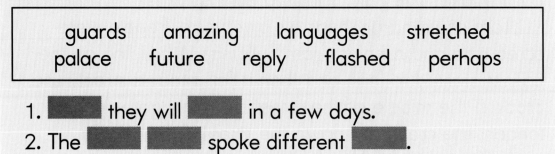

1. ▮▮▮ they will ▮▮▮ in a few days.
2. The ▮▮▮ ▮▮▮ spoke different ▮▮▮.

Write the word from the box that means the same thing as the underlined part of each sentence.

stern	finally	crouched	faded
forever	buckle	bow	

3. The <u>front</u> of the ship was damaged.
4. The smoke <u>slowly disappeared</u> in the gentle wind.
5. <u>At last</u>, he finished the book.

Review Items

6. Write the letters of the 4 names that tell about time.
7. Write the letters of the 4 names that tell about length or distance.
8. Write the letter of the one name that tells about temperature.
9. Write the letters of the 3 names that tell about speed.

    a. miles per hour

    b. miles

    c. hours

    d. yards

    e. centimeters per second

    f. weeks

    g. degrees

    h. minutes

    i. inches

    j. yards per minute

    k. years

    l. centimeters

The arrow on the handle shows which way it turns.
10. Which arrow shows the way the log moves?
11. Which arrow shows the way the vine moves?

12. Write the letter of the sun you see early in the morning.
13. Write the letter of the sun you see at sunset.
14. Write the letter of the sun you see at noon.

15. Airplanes land at airports. Ships land at ▆▆▆.

   • airports   • gates   • harbors

16. Airplanes are pulled by little trucks. Ships are pulled by ▆▆▆.

17. Airplanes unload at gates. Ships unload at ▆▆▆.

   • docks   • gates   • harbors

18. Which picture shows the smallest force?

19. Which picture shows the largest force?

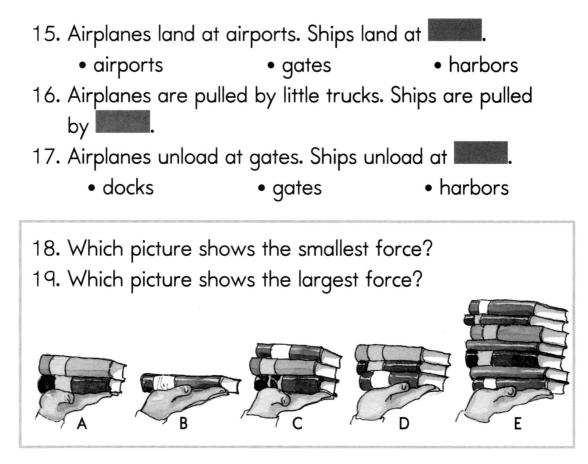

20. How many inches long is a yard?

21. About how many inches long is a meter?

A

1	2	3	4
1. electric	1. <u>for</u>ever	1. slaves	1. blade
2. computer	2. <u>pal</u>ace	2. rafts	2. Nile
3. appliance	3. <u>pock</u>et	3. queens	3. Egypt
4. pyramid	4. <u>sol</u>dier	4. buried	4. sword
	5. <u>flash</u>light	5. recorder	

B   **More About** Time

In today's story, you'll find out more about the trip that Eric and Tom took through time.

Touch dot B on the time line. That is the year Eric and Tom found the time machine.

Touch dot A. That's the year Thrig was from.

A ● The year Thrig was from

B ● Eric and Tom found the time machine.

C ● Eric and Tom were in San Francisco.

Touch dot C. That was the year Eric and Tom were in San Francisco.

You learned about things that were first made around the year 1900. Name those things.

C   Facts About Egypt

The story that you will read today tells about Egypt.
Egypt is a country that is close to Greece and Turkey.
Here are facts about Egypt:

- Egypt has a great river running through it. That river
is named the Nile. Touch the Nile River on the map.

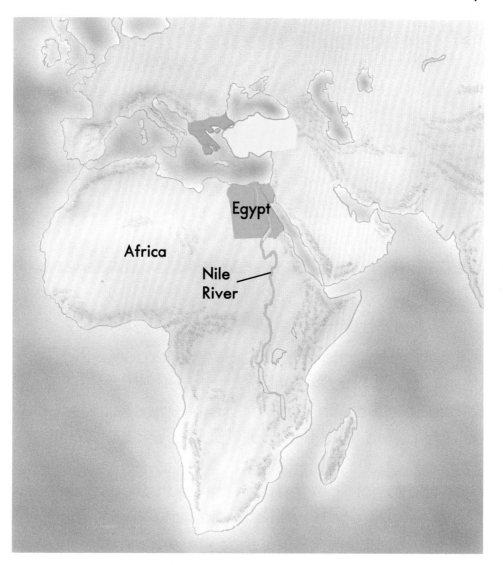

- Egypt is famous for its pyramids and palaces.
- Pyramids are huge stone buildings that are over five thousand years old. The picture shows pyramids.

- Dead kings and queens of Egypt were made into mummies and buried in pyramids.

D Eric and Tom in Egypt

Eric had fallen into the crack in the ground. But Tom held on to Eric's hand. Tom looked down into the crack. It seemed to go down forever. Tom almost slipped. He pulled and pulled, and he finally pulled Eric out of the crack.

Then they ran. They pushed through crowds. From time to time, the earth would shake and knock them down. They ran past houses that were burning. They ran past houses that had fallen over.

When the boys got to the mountain outside the city, they looked back as they ran. The whole city was burning. They could hear people screaming in the distance. The boys ran up the side of the mountain to the time machine.

After they caught their breath, Tom said, "Let's figure out a way to get back to the right time."

They went inside the time machine. Dials were clicking and lights were flashing inside the machine. Tom sat down in the seat. The door shut: "Swwwshshsh." Tom pointed to the handle that Eric had pulled. "This makes the time machine work," Tom said.

Eric said, "When I pulled down on it, we went back in time."

Tom said, "I'll bet we will go forward in time if we push the handle up."

"Push it up," Eric said.

Tom grabbed the handle. It felt very cold. He tried to push it up, but it wouldn't move. "It's stuck," he said. "The handle won't move."

Eric pushed on the handle, but the outcome was the same.

"It's got to move," Tom said. He pushed and pulled with all his strength. Suddenly, the handle moved down. A force pushed against him.

Eric's voice sounded far away as he said, "Oh, no."

Lights went on and off. Dials clicked and buzzed. Then things began to quiet down. Eric said, "I'm afraid to look outside."

Tom stood up. The door opened. It was very bright outside. At first, Tom couldn't believe what he saw.

The time machine was on the side of a mountain above a great river. There were  many rafts and boats on the river. But they did not look like any rafts or boats that Tom had ever seen before. Next to the river was a city. But it did not look like any city that Tom had ever seen before. All the buildings in the city were white. And next to the city were two great pyramids. One of them was already built and the other one was almost finished. Hundreds of men were dragging great stones toward this pyramid.

"We're in Egypt," Tom said. "We're in Egypt five thousand years ago! Look over there. The men are building a pyramid."

"What are pyramids for?" Eric asked.

Tom said, "When a king dies, they put him in a pyramid along with all of his slaves and his goats and everything else he owned."

Eric said, "Let's not leave the time machine now. We could take a nap. When it's dark, we'll go down to the city."

Tom and Eric slept. They woke up just as the sun was setting. Tom looked inside the time machine for a flashlight. He found one on a shelf. Next to it was a tiny tape recorder. He put the flashlight in one pocket and the tape recorder in the other.

Then Eric and Tom started down the mountain. They were very hungry. Down, down they went. They found a road at the bottom of the mountain. The road led into the city.

It was very quiet and very dark in the city. Tom took his flashlight out and was ready to turn it on when something happened.

MORE NEXT TIME

⸻

E **Number your paper from 1 through 14.**

1. Some buildings in Egypt are over ▉▉▉ years old.
   - 7 thousand   • 15 thousand   • 5 thousand
2. What is the name of the great river that runs through Egypt?

3. Which letter shows where Turkey is?
4. Which letter shows where Egypt is?
5. Which letter shows where the Nile River is?

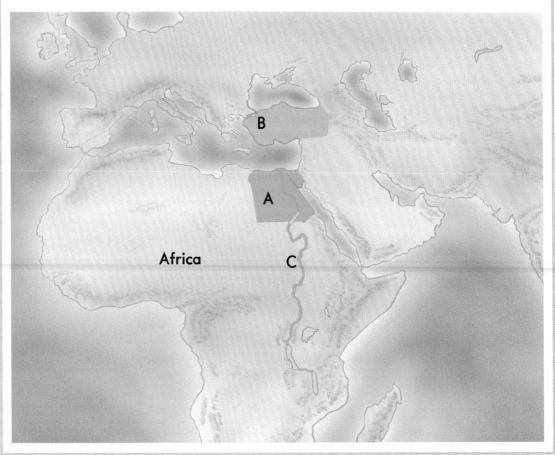

Review Items
6. The temperature inside your body is about 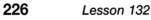 degrees when you are healthy.
7. Most fevers don't go over ▓▓▓▓ degrees.
8. Write the letters of the 4 years that are in the past.

a. 1980	c. 2100	e. 1947
b. 2010	d. 1897	f. 1994

9. Write the letters of the 9 places that are in the United States.

a. Italy
b. Ohio
c. China
d. Chicago
e. Alaska
f. Denver
g. San Francisco
h. Japan
i. California
j. Australia
k. Texas
l. Lake Michigan
m. Turkey
n. New York City
o. Canada

10. Write 3 years that are in the future.

11. What is it called when the sun comes up?

• sunrise   • sunset

12. What is it called when the sun goes down?

13. You would have the least power if you pushed against one of the handles. Which handle is that?

14. Which handle would give you the most amount of power?

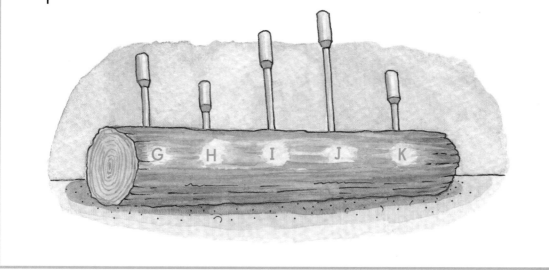

A

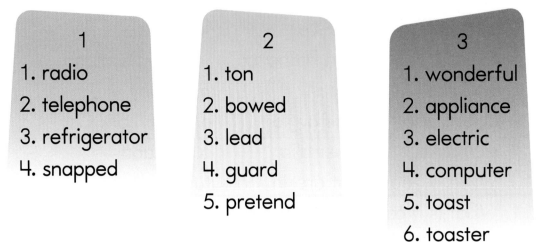

1
1. radio
2. telephone
3. refrigerator
4. snapped

2
1. ton
2. bowed
3. lead
4. guard
5. pretend

3
1. wonderful
2. appliance
3. electric
4. computer
5. toast
6. toaster

B   **More About** Time

Look at the time line.

Touch dot B. Dot B shows the year that Eric and Tom found the time machine. What year was that?

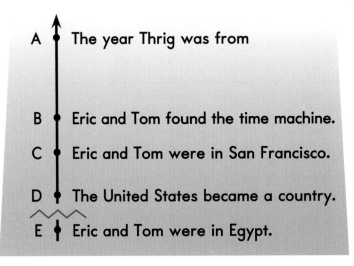

A ● The year Thrig was from

B ● Eric and Tom found the time machine.

C ● Eric and Tom were in San Francisco.

D ● The United States became a country.

E ● Eric and Tom were in Egypt.

Touch dot A. Dot A shows the year that Thrig was from. What year was that?

Touch dot C. Dot C shows the year that Eric and Tom were in San Francisco. When was that?

Touch dot D. Dot D shows the year that the United States became a country. What year was that?

Touch dot E. Dot E shows when Eric and Tom were in Egypt. How long ago was that?

C Eric and Tom Go to a Palace

Tom was ready to turn his flashlight on. Suddenly, a soldier was standing in front of him. The soldier had metal bands on his arms, and he held a large sword. He pointed the sword at Tom. "Ha hu ru," he said.

Tom looked at the soldier and said, "I don't know what you said."

The soldier moved the sword closer to Tom. Tom could see little marks on the blade. He could see a big scar on the soldier's hand. "Ha hu ru," the soldier said again.

Eric said, "He looks mad. We'd better do something."

The soldier yelled, "Ha hu ru," and shook his sword. But Tom still couldn't understand him.

The blade of the sword was only inches from Tom's face.

Tom put his hand over his face. He didn't remember that he had a flashlight in his hand. Without thinking, Tom turned it on.

When the soldier saw the light, he stepped back. He put his sword on the ground. "On kon urub," he said very softly. The soldier got down on his hands and knees. "On kon urub," he said again.

Eric said, "He thinks that you have some kind of great power. <u>Maybe</u> he thinks you are a <u>sun god</u>."

Tom smiled, "Maybe it will be fun to be a sun god."

Eric said, "Be careful, Tom."

Tom walked over to the soldier. "Take me to your <u>king,</u>" he said. "The sun god wants to meet the king of Egypt." Tom pointed toward the middle of the city.

The soldier stood up. He bowed three times. Then he started to lead the boys down the streets. Soon they came to a large palace that ⭐ had hundreds of steps in front of it.

The soldier went up to three guards who were in front of the palace. The soldier talked and pointed to Tom. Then one guard walked up to the boys. The guard backed away and bowed three times.

Eric said, "I think he wants us to follow him."

So Tom and Eric followed the guard. Up the steps they went. Up, up, up to the great doors that led inside the palace.

"What a palace," Tom said. He had never been in a building so big. The hall seemed blocks and blocks long. And a soldier was standing every two yards on each side of the hall. There were hundreds of soldiers in that hall.

The guard walked down the hall. Tom and Eric followed. At last they walked through another huge door. They were now inside a great room looking at an old man. He was sitting on the floor with a large chain around his neck. At the end of the chain was a large metal ball. The ball looked like the sun.

The soldier said something to the old man. The old man looked at the boys for a long time. Then he smiled and stood up. He walked over and held out his hand. "Ura bustu," he said.

"He wants the flashlight," Eric said. "Don't give it to him."

"Don't worry," Tom said. Tom shook his head no. Then he pointed the flashlight at the sun on the old man's neck chain. Tom turned the flashlight on. The sun became bright.

The old man held his hand over the sun. "On kon urub," he said. "On kon urub."

Eric said, "Now <u>he</u> thinks that you're a sun god."

MORE NEXT TIME

D Number your paper from 1 through 22.

Skill Items

Here are 3 events that happened in the story. Write **beginning, middle,** or **end** for each event.

1. A soldier led the boys to a palace.

2. Tom shined the flashlight on the old man's neck chain.

3. A soldier pointed a sword at Tom.

His argument convinced them to buy an appliance.

4. What word names a machine that's used around the house?

5. What word means he **made somebody believe something?**

6. What word refers to what he said to convince people?

Review Items

7. Which letter shows where Italy is?
8. Which letter shows where China is?
9. Which letter shows where Turkey is?
10. Which letter shows where Japan is?
11. Is the United States shown on this map?

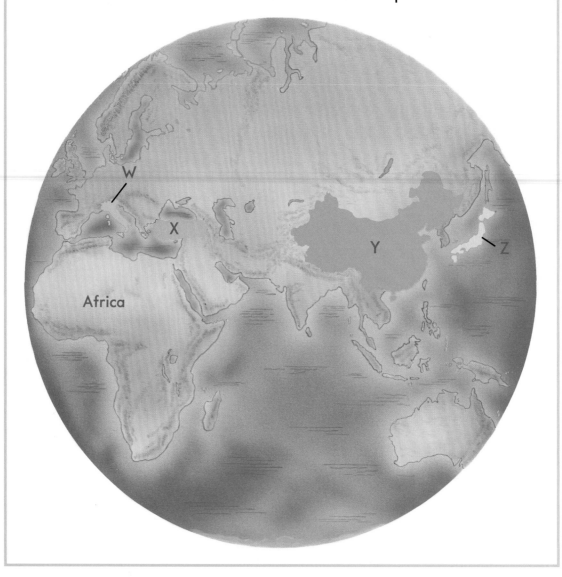

12. A plane that flies from Italy to New York City goes in which direction?

13. Some buildings in Egypt are over ▢ years old.
   • 20 thousand   • 5 thousand   • 8 thousand

14. When kings and queens of Egypt died, they were buried inside a ▢.

15. Write the letters of the 9 places that are in the United States.

    a. Denver   h. Japan
    b. Turkey   i. New York City
    c. Chicago   j. Texas
    d. China   k. San Francisco
    e. Alaska   l. Ohio
    f. Italy   m. California
    g. Lake Michigan   n. Egypt

16. A mile is a little more than ▢ feet.

17. What liquid does the **A** show?

18. What liquid does the **B** show?

19. What liquid does the **C** show?

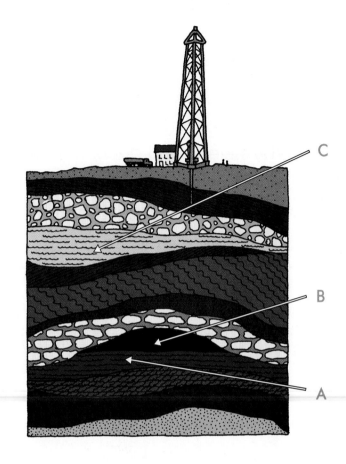

20. Which letter shows Turkey?

21. Which letter shows Egypt?

22. Which letter shows the Nile River?

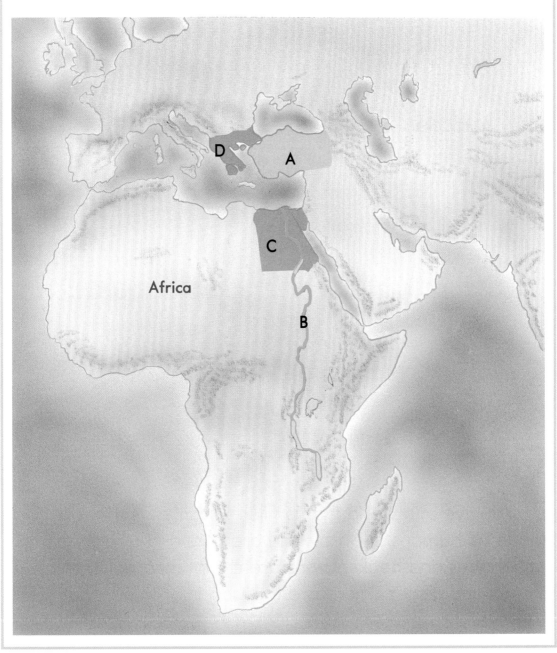

A

1
1. ancient
2. mammoth
3. throne
4. bowl
5. toaster
6. electric

2
1. <u>dish</u>washer
2. <u>app</u>liance
3. <u>gol</u>den
4. <u>in</u>sist
5. <u>tele</u>phone
6. <u>te</u>levision

3
1. spices
2. bulbs
3. radios
4. invention
5. refrigerators
6. computer

4
1. smashed
2. invented
3. snapped
4. pretended

B

Inventing

You live in a world that is filled with things that are made by humans. In this world are cars and airplanes and telephones and books. There are chairs and tables and stoves and dishes. There are thousands of things that you use every day.

Each of these things was **invented.** That means that somebody made the object for the first time. The person who made the first automobile invented the automobile. The person who made the first television invented the television. Remember, when somebody makes an object for the first time, the person invents that object. The object the person makes is called the invention. The first airplane was an invention. The first telephone was an invention.

Everything that is made by humans was invented by somebody. At one time, there were no cars, light bulbs, or glass windows. People didn't know how to make these things, because nobody had invented them yet.

Most of the things that you use every day were invented after the year 1800. Here are just some of the things that people did not have before 1800: trains, trucks, cars, airplanes, bicycles, telephones, radios, televisions, movies, tape recorders, computers, electric appliances like washing machines, toasters, refrigerators, or dishwashers.

C Eric and Tom Meet the King

Tom and Eric were in a huge palace. Tom had just convinced the old man with the golden sun that Tom was a sun god. The old man was holding his hand over the sun and saying, "On kon urub." Then the old man lifted the golden sun from around his neck and held it out for Tom. The old man bowed and said, "Ura, ura."

Eric said, "I think he wants you to have the golden sun."

Tom didn't want to take the sun, but the old man seemed to insist that he take it.

The sun was so heavy that Tom wondered how the old man could walk around with it hanging from his neck. Just as Tom put the chain around his neck, one of the guards handed him a pillow with a large gray cat sitting on it.

Eric said, "They think cats have special powers."

Tom felt silly with a large sun around his neck as he held a pillow with a gray cat on it.

Eric said, "I don't know about you, but I am very hungry."

Tom said, "Me, too." He handed the cat to the guard. Then he snapped his fingers. "Eat, eat," Tom said, and pretended to eat.

"Hem stroo," the soldier said smiling. "Hem stroo." The soldier ran from the room and down the hall.

Suddenly, many people came into the room. They were carrying all kinds of food. Tom looked at all of the food in front of him. He saw a large bowl. It had milk in it. Tom said, "I'll bet it's goat milk."

Eric tasted it. He made a face. "It's warm," he said. "Why don't they have cold milk?"

Tom said, "Their milk isn't cold because they don't have any way to keep it cold. Nobody had refrigerators until after the year 1800."

Tom and Eric ate and ate. Then the old man took Tom and Eric to their room. Tom put his flashlight in his pocket and went to sleep.

In the morning the old man took the boys to a great

room at the end of the hall. Inside the room a young man sat on a throne. The throne was made of gold and silver.

Eric said, "That young man must be the king."

"Hara uha <u>ho</u>," the king said. His voice was sharp.

Tom and Eric walked to the throne. The king stood up and walked to a window in the room. He pointed to the sunlight that was coming through the window. "Tasa u horu," he said. Then he pointed to Tom. "Umul hock a huck."

Tom knew what the king wanted. Tom pointed the flashlight at the king and pressed the button on the flashlight. But nothing happened. The flashlight did not go on. Tom pressed the button again. The outcome was the same.

"Aso uhuck," the king said. He snapped his fingers and two soldiers came forward. One of them grabbed Tom and the other grabbed Eric.

The king grabbed the flashlight from Tom's hand and threw it to the floor. It smashed. Tom looked at the flashlight. Then he looked up into the face of the king. The king looked very, very mean.

MORE NEXT TIME

Number your paper from 1 through 22.

Skill Items

Write the word from the box that means the same thing as the underlined part of each sentence.

survived	damaged	lowered	rescued
woven	clomping	fixed	dull	center

1. Jane <u>saved</u> the child from the river.
2. Tom <u>broke</u> the bicycle when he ran over the rock.
3. She thinks that book is <u>boring</u>.

Use the words in the box to write complete sentences.

convinced	languages	modern	discovered	palace
argument	countries	dirty	guards	appliance

4. The ▩▩ ▩▩ spoke different ▩▩.
5. His ▩▩ ▩▩ them to buy an ▩▩.

Review Items

6. Airplanes land at airports. Ships land at ▩▩.
   • gates   • airports   • harbors
7. Airplanes are pulled by little trucks. Ships are pulled by ▩▩.
8. Airplanes unload at gates. Ships unload at ▩▩.
   • harbors   • docks   • gates

9. What is the temperature of the water in each jar?

10. Write the letter of each jar that is filled with ocean water.

11. Jar C is filled with ocean water. How do you know?

32 degrees 32 degrees 32 degrees 32 degrees 32 degrees 32 degrees

A   B   C   D   E   F

12. Which is longer, a yard or a meter?

13. Which is longer, a centimeter or a meter?

14. How many centimeters are in a meter?

15. In 1906, most of the streets in San Francisco were made of _____. • bricks   • steel   • dirt

16. The streetlights were _____. • not as bright • brighter

17. Most of the houses were made of _____.

18. Write the letters of the 3 items that tell how people got from place to place.

    a. airplanes   c. wagons   e. trucks

    b. bikes   d. horses   f. buses

19. During the San Francisco earthquake, fires started when the _____ lines broke.

20. What made the street crack?

21. Where did Eric and Tom go after leaving San Francisco?

22. In Egypt, how did Tom try to show he was a sun god?

A

1	2
1. language	1. spices
2. argue	2. grain
3. saber-toothed	3. further
4. mammoth	4. scratching
5. ancient	5. replied

B

Eric and Tom Leave Egypt

A soldier was holding Tom. The flashlight was on the floor. It was broken. Tom could not play sun god anymore.

The king was yelling at the old man. Suddenly, Tom got an idea. He reached into his pocket and took out the tape recorder. He pressed the button. The king was saying, "Ra hu hub haki."

Tom held the tape recorder up high and played back what he had recorded. "Ra hu hub haki." The king stopped yelling. He looked at Tom. The soldier let go of Tom. Tom ran the tape back and played it again. He played it as loud as it would go. "Ra hu hub haki."

The king smiled and bowed. Tom walked up to the king. He pressed the button so that the tape recorder would record again. Then he said, "I am the sun god, and I have your words on this tape."

The king bowed and said, "Un uh, run duh."

Tom played the tape back as loud as he could.

Eric said, "Tom, let's get out of here before the tape recorder breaks. Remember what happened to the flashlight."

Eric and Tom walked down the long, long hall. They did not look back. They walked through the great doors of the palace. Then they started to run. They ran down the stairs—down, down. When they came to the bottom of the stairs, they kept on running. They ran down the streets of the city until they came to the river. Then they stopped. They were both tired. People around them were pointing at them and talking, but Tom and Eric felt safe here.

Tom said, "That's the Nile River." He pointed to one of the huge rafts on the river. "That raft is carrying hundreds and hundreds of sacks of grain." Tom continued, "One raft can carry as much grain as a hundred wagons could carry."

"Why don't they use trucks?" Eric asked.

Tom laughed. "Nobody will have trucks in Egypt for thousands of years."

Eric looked at the rafts on the river. They carried all kinds of things—animals, furs, spices, food, and even great big stones the size of a car. "What are they going to do with those stones?" he asked.

Tom said, "They will use them to build a pyramid. They need thousands of stones to build one pyramid."

Just then a soldier came up to Eric and Tom. He held out his sword. "Ra uh hack stuck," he said.

Tom held up the tape recorder and played back the soldier's words. "Ra uh hack stuck." The soldier backed away.

Tom and Eric found a path that led up the mountain. They walked up and up. The mountain was very steep, and by the time they got to the time machine, they were tired and hungry.

They went inside the time machine. Tom sat down in the seat. "This time," he said, "I'm going to make the handle go <u>up</u> so we can go <u>forward</u> in time."

"I hope so," Eric said. "I don't want to go back any further in time."

Tom pushed up on the handle. It did not move. He moved in the seat. Then, suddenly, the handle moved up. Dials started to click and buzz. Lights went on and off. Tom felt the force against his face.

Then everything was quiet except for a few dials that were clicking and buzzing. Tom heard something scratching on the outside of the time machine. He stood up. The door opened. And something started to walk inside the time machine. It was a great big yellow lion.

MORE NEXT TIME

C Number your paper from 1 through 21.

Write the years for the things shown on this time line.

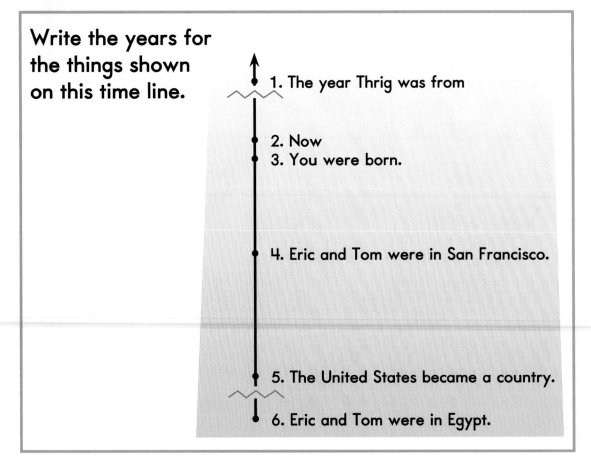

1. The year Thrig was from

2. Now
3. You were born.

4. Eric and Tom were in San Francisco.

5. The United States became a country.

6. Eric and Tom were in Egypt.

Skill Items

Write the word from the box that means the same thing as the underlined part of each sentence.

ocean	always	pilot	attention	several
although	globe	galley	whole	

7. The plane's <u>kitchen</u> was very dirty.
8. He stayed home, <u>but</u> he wanted to go to the party.
9. She gave me <u>more than two</u> books to read.

Review Items

10. Write the letter that shows a tugboat.
11. Write 2 letters that show ships.
12. Write 2 letters that show docks.

13. In what year did Tom and Eric see the San Francisco earthquake?

14. When kings and queens of Egypt died, they were buried inside a ▮▮▮▮.

15. Some buildings in Egypt are over ▮▮▮▮ years old.
    • 5 thousand   • 10 thousand   • 15 thousand

16. When a person makes an object for the first time, the person ▮▮▮▮ the object.

17. Write the letter of each thing that was not invented by somebody.

    a. television   f. trains
    b. flowers   g. bushes
    c. grass   h. cows
    d. toasters   i. tables
    e. spiders   j. dogs

18. Most of the things that we use every day were invented after the year ▮▮▮▮.
    • 2000   • 1900   • 1800

19. What is it called when the sun goes down?
    • sunrise   • sunset

20. What is it called when the sun comes up?
    • sunrise   •sunset

21. **Write the letter** of each thing that was invented after 1800.

    a. dishwashers   e. buildings   i. rafts
    b. cars   f. computers   j. flashlights
    c. doors   g. hats   k. swords
    d. pyramids   h. chairs

A

1	2	3
1. <u>re</u>plied	1. tame	1. gift
2. <u>ar</u>gue	2. war	2. stared
3. <u>door</u>way	3. deal	3. ancient
4. <u>lan</u>guage	4. spike	4. trumpet
5. <u>ar</u>my	5. tusk	

B

A Queen Named Helen

In today's story, you'll read more about the country of Greece three thousand years ago. At that time, part of Greece was at war with Troy. The war began because a Greek queen named Helen ran away with a man from Troy. One thousand ships left Greece to go to war against Troy. The war lasted for ten years, but the Greek army could not get inside the walls around Troy.

The war ended when the soldiers from Greece tricked the army from Troy. The Greek soldiers built a large horse and pretended to leave it as a gift. Then the army pretended to leave. The soldiers from Troy took the great horse inside the walls of the city. Greek soldiers were hiding inside the horse. That night, they came out, opened the gates, and let the army from Greece inside the city.

C   Eric and Tom in Greece

A lion was in the doorway of the time machine. The lion was walking toward Tom. Tom could see the muscles in the lion's legs as it walked.

Suddenly, a man came through the doorway of the time machine. He was wearing a long white robe. He stared at the lights and dials. The man put his hand on the lion's back. The lion looked up at the man.

"That lion is tame," Eric said.

The man said something to Tom and Eric, but they could not understand the man's language. The man pointed toward the door of the time machine and then walked out of the time machine. Tom and Eric followed him.

The time machine was in a place that looked like a park. There were trees and grass. A few young men were standing and talking. Tom said, "I think we are in a school of long, long ago. I think we are in ancient Greece."

Eric said, "I thought we went forward in time."

Tom said, "Maybe we did, but not far enough."

The man in the robe said something and then pointed to a large table covered with food. "He wants us to eat," Tom said.

"Good deal," Eric said. "I'm really hungry. I don't even care if they give us warm milk."

After Tom and Eric ate, they watched the young men and their teacher. The teacher sat on a stone bench. The young men sat on the ground around him. The teacher asked questions. The young men would try to answer the questions. The teacher asked more questions.

Tom said, "I think they're learning how to argue. They argue so they can learn to think clearly. The teacher wants to show them that they don't know as much as they think they know."

"Why is he doing that?" Eric asked.

Tom replied, "So they will think about things."

Just then a man on a horse rode to the top of a hill near the school. ⭐ Then he called to the teacher. The teacher walked up the hill. Tom and Eric followed. Tom could see the ocean from the top of the hill. The man on the horse pointed to hundreds of ships on the ocean.

Tom and Eric looked at the ships. Eric said, "I have never seen so many ships in one place before. Where do you think they're going?"

Tom said, "I think we're in Greece three thousand years

ago. A queen of one city in Greece ran away with somebody from Troy. So part of Greece went to war and sent a thousand ships into battle." Tom pointed to the ships below. "I think those are the ships that are going to Troy."

Some ships were loaded with soldiers and horses. Others carried large machines for throwing rocks through the air. Tom said, "Thousands of men will die in the battle with Troy. And that battle will go on for many years."

In the distance, Tom and Eric could hear the sounds of soldiers singing. Tom and Eric watched for a few minutes. The teacher standing next to them shook his head. He looked very sad.

"I think we'd better get out of here," Tom said. "I want to get back home."

Tom and Eric started to walk back to the time machine. The teacher and the young men were still on the hill.

Tom and Eric went inside the time machine. Tom sat down in the seat. The door closed. Then Tom said, "I wish I knew how to make this time machine work right."

Eric said, "Let _me_ try. You didn't do very well the last time _you_ tried."

Eric reached for the handle. Tom tried to push Eric's hand away, but Eric had a good grip on the handle. Suddenly, the handle moved down—almost all the way down. Before Tom could pull the handle back up, he felt the force against his face and ears.

"Oh, no!" Eric yelled. Then everything seemed to go dark.

MORE NEXT TIME

D Number your paper from 1 through 22.

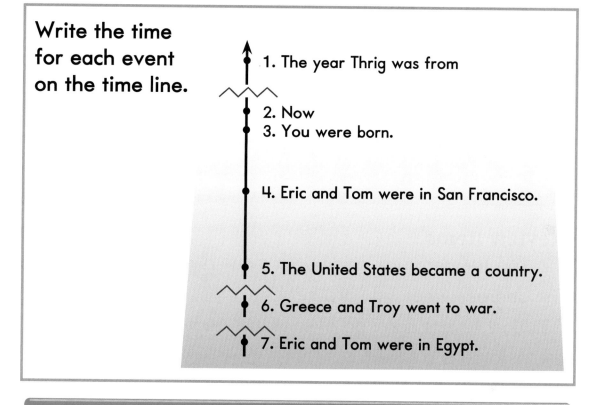

Write the time for each event on the time line.

1. The year Thrig was from
2. Now
3. You were born.
4. Eric and Tom were in San Francisco.
5. The United States became a country.
6. Greece and Troy went to war.
7. Eric and Tom were in Egypt.

Skill Items

Write the word from the box that means the same thing as the underlined part of each sentence.

completely	steel	supposed	lowered
fish	boiled	moist	buried	tadpoles

8. She counted hundreds of <u>baby toads</u>.
9. His clothes were <u>slightly wet</u> from the rain.
10. Jan's bedroom was <u>totally</u> clean.

11. Compare object A and object B. Remember, first tell how they're the same. Then tell how they're different.

Object A   Object B

Review Items

12. The temperature inside your body is about ▨▨▨▨ degrees when you are healthy.

13. Most fevers don't go over ▨▨▨▨ degrees.

14. A force is a ▨▨▨▨.

15. In Egypt, how did Tom try to show that he was a sun god?

16. When a person makes an object for the first time, the person ▨▨▨▨ the object.

17. In Egypt, Eric and Tom saw some huge stones on rafts. What were the stones for?

18. Why didn't the people in Egypt use trucks to haul things?

19. Which letter shows where Italy is?
20. Which letter shows where Egypt is?
21. Which letter shows where Greece is?
22. Which letter shows where Turkey is?

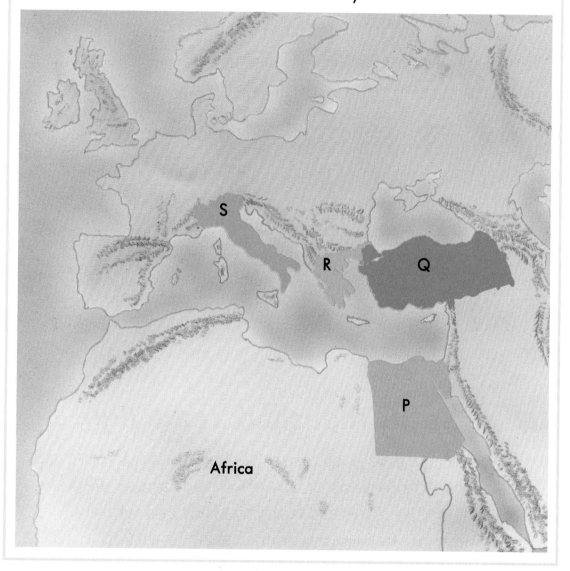

A

1
1. English
2. discover
3. future
4. brought
5. village
6. defeat

2
1. trumpeting
2. snorting
3. breathing
4. closing
5. crunching

3
1. tusks
2. charged
3. ponies
4. blinked

4
1. curved
2. tigers
3. spikes
4. modern
5. Spain

B **Forty Thousand Years Ago**

Things looked very different forty thousand years ago. There were no buildings or streets. The humans who lived then were a little different from the humans who live today. Some of them wore animal skins and lived in caves.

Many kinds of animals that you see today were around forty thousand years ago, but some of the animals from that time were different. The picture shows a saber-toothed tiger, a horse, a human, and a kind of elephant called a mammoth.

The saber-toothed tiger had a short tail and teeth like spikes.

The horse was much smaller than most horses of today.

The mammoth had long hair and long, curved tusks.

C Eric and Tom See Cave People

The force was so great that Tom's ears began ringing. He had trouble breathing. He couldn't talk. Then things inside the time machine looked brighter again. The dials and lights blinked and flashed.

"I hate to look outside," Eric said. His voice sounded funny.

Tom rubbed his eyes. "That handle went down almost all the way," Tom said.

Eric stood up and the door opened. The air was cool, and the trees outside looked a little different from any Tom had ever seen.

Eric and Tom stood outside the time machine for a few minutes. They looked in all directions, but they couldn't see any people. At first they didn't see any animals either. But then they heard a terrible roar.

A moment later, three very small horses charged down a hill. They were no bigger than ponies, but they looked different.

The horses ran through the long grass. Another animal was running behind them. It was very fast, but not as tall as the horses. Tom could see it leaping through the tall grass, but he couldn't get a good look at it. Suddenly, the horses turned and ran downhill. The animal that had been chasing them stopped and stood on top of a mound. Now Tom and Eric could see the animal clearly.

Eric said, "Do you see what I see?"

Tom didn't take his eyes from the animal. "Yes," he said.

The animal had a short tail, and two long teeth that stuck down like spikes. Tom said, "I think we've gone back about forty thousand years from our time. I think we're looking at a saber-toothed tiger."

Tom said, "Those other animals were horses that lived forty thousand years ago."

Just as Eric started to say something, a loud snorting noise came from the other side of the time machine. The boys turned around. The animal making the noise was

a giant mammoth—an elephant with long fur and great tusks. It held its trunk high in the air. Its eyes were bright and it didn't look friendly. "Let's get out of here," Tom said. The boys ducked inside the time machine. Tom ran to the seat and sat down, but just as the door was closing, the mammoth charged into it. It made a terrible crunching sound. And the door wouldn't close. The door was open about a foot. The mammoth stuck its trunk through the open door and let out a great trumpeting sound.

The mammoth suddenly backed up and began to run. Some humans were running down the hill. The humans were dressed in animal skins. They were shouting as they ran.

The mammoth ran downhill. "Let's get out of here," Tom said.

The humans were coming closer to the time machine. They were about fifty yards away. They were shouting and growling. Tom had picked up a long branch. He was trying to bend the door so that it would close.

Two men were running toward the door. "Push on the door," Tom yelled. He was trying to bend the bottom of the door with the branch.

The men were only a few yards from the door now. Tom could smell them. "Push," Tom said. "Push."

"Blump." One of the men had thrown a rock and hit the side of the time machine. "Blump, blump, blump." More rocks.

One of the men grabbed the door. Tom could see his face and his teeth.

MORE NEXT TIME

D Number your paper from 1 through 24.

Story Items

Here are the names of the animals you read about: **mammoth, saber-toothed tiger, horse.** Write the name of each animal.

1.   2.   3.

Write the time for each event on the time line.

4. The year Thrig was from

5. Now

6. You were born.

7. Eric and Tom were in San Francisco.

8. The United States became a country.

9. Greece and Troy went to war.

10. Eric and Tom were in Egypt.

11. Eric and Tom saw a saber-toothed tiger.

Review Items

12. **Write the letters** of the 2 years that are in the future.

a. 1980   c. 1890   e. 2090

b. 2140   d. 1750   f. 1990

13. Write the letter of the one name that tells about temperature.

14. Write the letters of the 2 names that tell about speed.

15. Write the letters of the 4 names that tell about time.

16. Write the letters of the 4 names that tell about distance or length.

a. centimeters

b. minutes

c. years

d. inches

e. miles

f. weeks

g. degrees

h. yards per month

i. hours

j. miles per hour

k. meters

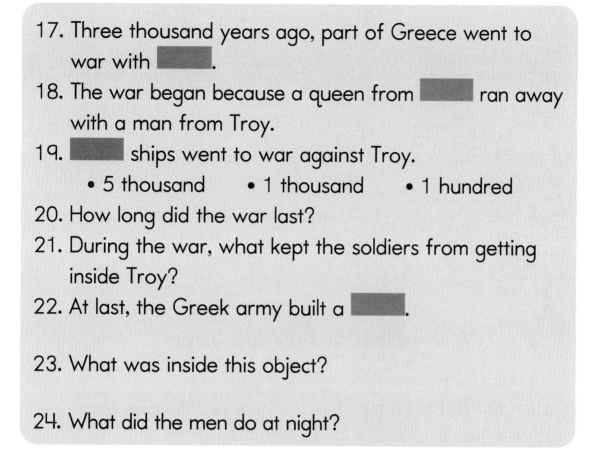

17. Three thousand years ago, part of Greece went to war with ▆▆▆▆.

18. The war began because a queen from ▆▆▆▆ ran away with a man from Troy.

19. ▆▆▆▆ ships went to war against Troy.

- 5 thousand   • 1 thousand   • 1 hundred

20. How long did the war last?

21. During the war, what kept the soldiers from getting inside Troy?

22. At last, the Greek army built a ▆▆▆▆.

23. What was inside this object?

24. What did the men do at night?

A

1
1. America
2. Mexico
3. Canada
4. Viking
5. Columbus

2
1. modern
2. brought
3. future
4. languages

3
1. defeated
2. village
3. discovered
4. English

B   More About Time

Look at the time line. Touch dot B. That dot shows when Eric and Tom started their trip. What year was that?

Touch dot A. That dot shows the year that Thrig was from. What year was that?

Touch dot C. That dot shows when Eric and Tom were in San Francisco. What year was that?

Touch dot D. That

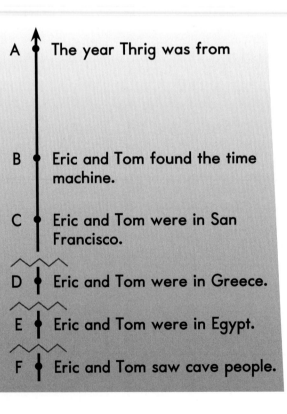

A — The year Thrig was from

B — Eric and Tom found the time machine.

C — Eric and Tom were in San Francisco.

D — Eric and Tom were in Greece.

E — Eric and Tom were in Egypt.

F — Eric and Tom saw cave people.

dot shows when Eric and Tom were in Greece. How long ago was that?

Touch dot E. That dot shows when Eric and Tom were in Egypt. How long ago was that?

Touch dot F. That dot shows when Eric and Tom saw the cave people. How long ago was that?

C   Eric and Tom in the City of the Future

"Push," Tom yelled. Just then a large rock hit the door. And suddenly the door closed. The rock must have straightened the door so that it could close again.

The door started to open again. "Quick," Tom said. "Sit in the chair so the door closes."

Eric ran to the seat and sat down. The door stayed closed now.

"Blump, blump." Rocks were hitting the side of the time machine.

"Push the handle up," Tom said. Eric bounced around in the seat and pushed on the handle. Rocks continued to hit the time machine.

Suddenly, the handle went up—far up. Tom almost fell down from the force. Then he almost passed out.

After a few moments, the force died down. Eric stood up, and the door opened.

The time machine was next to a huge building—the

tallest building that Tom had ever seen. There were buildings all around. Tom could not see the sun, only buildings. There were no streets and no cars—just buildings.

People were walking near the time machine. They wore funny clothes that seemed to shine.

Eric said, "We must have gone into the future."

A young man walked by the time machine. Tom said, "Can you help us?" The man looked at Tom and said, "Sellip." Then he walked away.

Tom and Eric stopped person after person. But every person said, "Sellip," and walked away. Finally, Tom stopped an old man. "Can you help us?" Tom asked.

The old man smiled. Very slowly he said, "I . . . will . . . try."

Tom and Eric grinned. Tom said, "Can you help us work our time machine?"

The old man made a face. Then he said, "Talk . . . slower."

Tom said, "Can . . . you . . . help . . . us . . . work . . . this . . . machine?"

The old man said, "No. We . . . have . . . machines . . . that ⭐ . . . fix . . . machines. People . . . do . . . not . . . fix machines."

Tom said, "Can . . . you . . . get . . . a machine . . . to help . . . us . . . work . . . our . . . time machine?"

The old man said, "That . . . time machine . . . is too old. We do not have . . . machines . . . that work . . . on such . . . old . . . time machines."

Tom felt sad. He and Eric would have to figure out how to work the machine by themselves.

The old man made a face. He thought for a few moments. Then he said, "What . . . year . . . are you . . . from?" Eric told him.

The old man thought and thought. "We . . . are . . . four thousand years . . . after your . . . time."

Eric said, "Why . . . do you speak . . . English? Nobody else . . . speaks . . . English."

The old man said, "I study . . . old, old languages. You . . . are very . . . lucky . . . to find me. No . . . other . . . people in the city . . . know . . . your language."

Eric asked, "What does . . . sellip . . . mean?"

The old man said, "Sellip . . . means this: I am . . . very sorry . . . that I cannot . . . help you. I . . . do not understand . . . your words. Good day."

Tom said, "Do you mean . . . that . . . one little . . . word . . . like sellip . . . means all that?"

"Yes," the old man said. "People . . . who live . . . in this time . . . do not have . . . to think . . . very much. So . . . the language . . . that they use . . . is very . . . simple. They . . . let the machines . . . do all . . . of their . . . thinking . . . for them."

Eric and Tom got into the time machine. Tom sat down and the door closed. Tom pulled the handle about halfway down. The dials buzzed. Lights went on and off. The force pushed against Tom's ears. Then it died down.

Tom stood up. The door opened. And outside the door, Tom could see water. On that water was a ship. But it wasn't a modern ship. It was an old-time sailing ship.

MORE NEXT TIME

D Number your paper from 1 through 21.

Skill Items

Write the word from the box that means the same thing as the underlined part of each sentence.

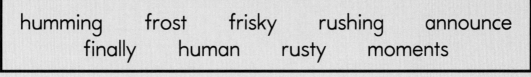

| humming | frost | frisky | rushing | announce |
| finally | human | rusty | moments |

1. Many <u>people</u> were waiting for the train.
2. She watched the <u>playful</u> kittens at the pet shop.
3. The water was <u>moving fast</u> over the rocks.

Review Items

4. **Write the letter** of each thing that was invented after 1800.

   a. televisions   e. buildings   i. rafts
   b. cars   f. computers   j. flashlights
   c. doors   g. hats   k. swords
   d. telephones   h. chairs

5. Three thousand years ago, part of Greece went to war with ▪▪▪▪▪.

6. How long did the war last?

7. During the war between part of Greece and Troy, what kept the soldiers from getting inside Troy?

8. At last, the Greek army built a ▪▪▪▪▪.

9. What was inside this object?

10. What did the men in that object do at night?

11. Write the letters of the 5 names that tell about time.

12. Write the letters of the 6 names that tell about distance or length.

13. Write the letter of the one name that tells about temperature.

14. Write the letters of the 3 names that tell about speed.

a. degrees
b. minutes
c. inches per year
d. years
e. miles per hour
f. weeks
g. centimeters
h. hours

i. miles
j. meters
k. feet per second
l. inches
m. feet
n. yards
o. days

15. Write the letters of **3** things that were true of humans 40 thousand years ago.

    a. They were taller than people of today.

    b. They were shorter than people of today.

    c. They lived in caves.

    d. They wore hats.

    e. They wore animal skins.

    f. They rode bikes.

    g. They lived in buildings.

    h. They lived in pyramids.

    i. They drove cars.

16. Write the letters that tell about a mammoth.

17. Write the letters that tell about an elephant of today.

    a. short hair   c. long hair

    b. short tusks   d. long tusks

18. Write the letters that tell about a saber-toothed tiger.

19. Write the letters that tell about a tiger of today.

    a. short tail   c. long tail   e. long teeth

    b. no teeth   d. no ears   f. short teeth

20. During the San Francisco earthquake, fires started when the ▓▓▓▓ lines broke.

21. What made the street crack?

A

1	2
1. Mexico	1. Columbus
2. discovered	2. brought
3. America	3. Canada
4. angry	4. crouch
5. countries	5. Spain
6. Vikings	6. crouched

B

More About Time

Look at the time line. Touch dot C. That dot shows when Eric and Tom started their trip. What year was that?

Touch dot A. That dot shows when Eric and Tom were in the city of the future. How far in the future was that?

Touch dot B. That dot shows the year that Thrig was from. What year was that?

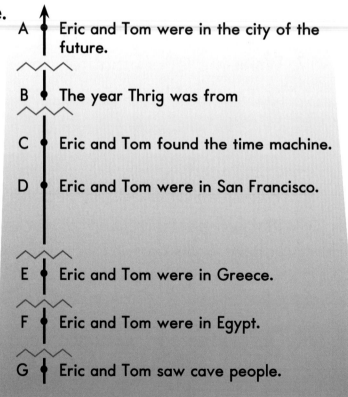

A — Eric and Tom were in the city of the future.

B — The year Thrig was from

C — Eric and Tom found the time machine.

D — Eric and Tom were in San Francisco.

E — Eric and Tom were in Greece.

F — Eric and Tom were in Egypt.

G — Eric and Tom saw cave people.

Touch dot D. That dot shows when Eric and Tom were in San Francisco. What year was that?

Touch dot E. That dot shows when Eric and Tom were in Greece. How long ago was that?

Touch dot F. That dot shows when Eric and Tom were in Egypt. How long ago was that?

Touch dot G. That dot shows when Eric and Tom saw the cave people. How long ago was that?

C North America

In today's story, you will read about North America. Here are some countries that are in North America: Canada, the United States, and Mexico.

See if you can name those three countries that are in North America.

Touch each country on the map.

Remember, the United States is part of North America. But North America is bigger than the United States.

Spain in 1492

Tom and Eric were near an ocean. In the distance they could see an old-time sailing ship. There was a shack near the shore. Tom and Eric started down the hill toward the shack. A fat man standing next to the shack was wearing funny pants and a long cape. The man called out to Tom, but Tom couldn't understand what he said. Tom called, "Do you speak English?"

The man replied, "Yes."

Tom walked down to the shack. Eric followed him. Tom said, "What year is it?"

The man said, "1492."

Eric said, "Wasn't that the year that Columbus discovered America?"

"Yes," Tom said. "Columbus discovered America in 1492."

The man became angry. "Did you say Columbus?" The man pointed to the ship at the dock. "That ship belongs to Columbus. Columbus is a crazy person."

The man went into his shack. Tom and Eric followed. On the walls were many maps, but they did not look like any maps that Tom and Eric had ever seen.

The man touched a spot on the largest map. "We are here in Spain. Columbus plans to sail his ships off the end of the world. He says that the world is round, but it is flat. If the world was round,  we would roll off."

Eric said, "Everybody knows that the world is round."

The man shouted, "You lie. I am going to call the soldiers."

Tom took out the tape recorder. Then he said to the man, "Say something. Say anything at all."

The man said, "I will take you to the soldiers."

Tom played back what the man had said. "I will take you to the soldiers."

The man looked around the room. "Who said that?" He looked at the recorder. "A voice without a man!"

Tom explained the tape recorder. Then Eric said, "That big thing on the hill is our time machine. It brought us here."

The man shook his head. Then he said, "You know things that I do not know. Why does the world look so flat if it is round?"

Tom pointed to a ship that was far out on the ocean. "Look at that ship. All you can see is the top part of it."

The man looked at the ship. "You are right," he said. "I cannot see the bottom part of the ship."

Tom said, "You cannot see the bottom part of the ship because the earth is round. If the earth were flat, you would be able to see the whole ship. The earth looks flat because it is very, very big. You see just a small part of it."

Then Eric said, "Tom, I just saw something go into our time machine."

"What was it?" Tom asked.

Eric replied, "It looked like a big white dog."

The man hit his fist on the table. "I would like to kill that dog. He is mean. And he always comes around my shack. He bit one of my men the other day."

Eric said, "What if that dog bumps against the handle? We'll never get home."

Eric and Tom ran from the shack. They ran up the hill to the time machine. The fat man was right behind them.

MORE NEXT TIME

 **Number your paper from 1 through 25.**

Write the time for each event shown on the time line.
- 4 thousand years in the future
- 40 thousand years ago
- 3 thousand years ago

1. Eric and Tom were in the city of the future.

2. The year Thrig was from

3. Now

4. You were born.

5. Eric and Tom were in San Francisco.

6. The United States became a country.

7. Greece and Troy went to war.

8. Eric and Tom were in Egypt.

9. Eric and Tom saw a saber-toothed tiger.

10. Write the letters of 3 places that are in North America.

    a. Japan   c. Mexico   e. Canada
    b. the United States   d. Greece   f. Italy

11. Write the letters of 2 places that are in the United States.

    a. Japan   c. Italy   e. Ohio
    b. Mexico   d. San Francisco   f. Canada

Story Items

12. Let's say you saw a ship far out on the ocean. Would you be able to see the **whole ship** or just the **top part?**

13. Would you see **more** of the ship or **less** of the ship if the world was flat?

Review Items

14. Could all the people in the city of the future understand Eric and Tom?

15. Why could the old man understand them?

16. The people in the city of the future did not fix their machines. What fixed their machines?

17. The people of the future used such a simple language because ▮▮▮▮.

    • They were very smart.
    • They didn't think much.
    • They didn't like people.

18. In 1906, most of the streets in San Francisco were made of ███.

       • tar   • dirt   • brick

19. Most of the houses were made of ███.

20. The streetlights were ███.

       • not as bright   • brighter

21. Write the letters of the items that tell how people got from place to place.

    a. airplanes   c. wagons   e. trucks

    b. bikes   d. horses   f. buses

22. Which letter shows a horse from 40 thousand years ago?

23. Which letter shows a saber-toothed tiger?

24. Which letter shows a mammoth?

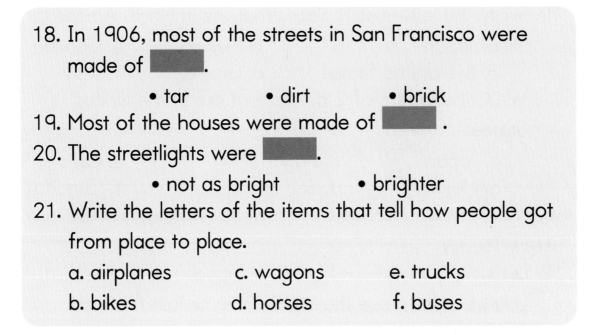

J   K   R

25. Where did Eric and Tom go after they left the cave people?

Number your paper from 1 through 36.

1. Write the letters of the 3 years that are in the future.

a. 2099 c. 1990 e. 2020
b. 1888 d. 1699 f. 2220

2. Write the letters of the 5 names that tell about time.

3. Write the letters of the 6 names that tell about distance or length.

4. Write the letters of the 2 names that tell about speed.

a. days
b. minutes
c. centimeters
d. inches
e. weeks
f. meters
g. degrees

h. feet
i. hours
j. miles per hour
k. miles
l. centimeters per day
m. yards
n. years

5. Some buildings in Egypt are over ▓▓▓ years old.

• 20 thousand   •10 thousand   • 5 thousand

6. What is the name of the great river that runs through Egypt?

7. When kings and queens of Egypt died, they were buried inside a ▓▓▓.

8. When a person makes an object for the first time, the person ▓▓▓ the object.

9. Which letter shows where Turkey is?
10. Which letter shows where Greece is?
11. Which letter shows where Italy is?
12. Which letter shows where Spain is?
13. Which letter shows where Egypt is?

14. **Write the letters** of the 5 things that were invented after 1800.

a. pyramids   e. buildings   i. bicycles
b. airplanes   f. clothing   j. flashlights
c. doors   g. rafts   k. swords
d. tape recorders h. movies

15. Three thousand years ago, part of Greece went to war with ▮▮▮▮.

16. The war began because a queen from ▮▮▮▮ ran away with a man from ▮▮▮▮.

17. ▮▮▮▮ ships went to war with Troy.

• 5 hundred   • 1 thousand   • 2 thousand

18. How long did the war last?

19. Write the letters that tell about a mammoth.

a. long tusks   c. short tusks
b. long hair   d. short hair

20. Write the letters that tell about a saber-toothed tiger.

a. no ears   c. no teeth   e. long teeth
b. long tail   d. short tail

21. Write the letters of the 9 places that are in the United States.

a. Italy   f. Denver   k. Lake Michigan
b. Turkey   g. Ohio   l. New York
c. Chicago   h. California   m. Egypt
d. China   i. Texas   n. Spain
e. Alaska   j. San Francisco o. Greece

Write the time for each event shown on the time line.

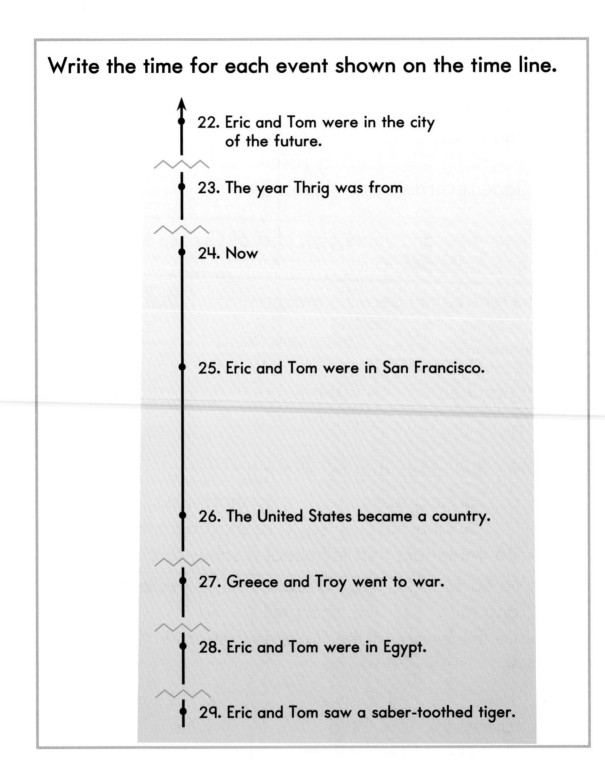

22. Eric and Tom were in the city of the future.

23. The year Thrig was from

24. Now

25. Eric and Tom were in San Francisco.

26. The United States became a country.

27. Greece and Troy went to war.

28. Eric and Tom were in Egypt.

29. Eric and Tom saw a saber-toothed tiger.

30. Is the world round or flat?

31. Did Columbus think that the world was round or flat?

Skill Items

For each item, write the underlined word from the sentences in the box.

The <u>palace</u> <u>guards</u> spoke different <u>languages</u>.
His <u>argument</u> <u>convinced</u> them to buy an <u>appliance</u>.

32. What underlining names the place where a king and queen live?

33. What underlining means he made somebody believe something?

34. What underlining names a machine that's used around the house?

35. What underlining refers to the words that people use to say things?

36. What underlining refers to what he said to convince people?

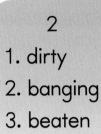

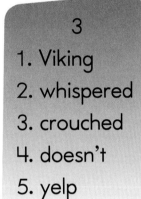

1	2	3
1. George Washington	1. dirty	1. Viking
2. probably	2. banging	2. whispered
3. attack	3. beaten	3. crouched
4. Concord	4. sniffed	4. doesn't
5. president		5. yelp

B More About Time

Look at the time line. Touch dot C. That dot shows when Eric and Tom started their trip. What year was that?

Touch dot A. That dot shows when Eric and Tom were in the city of the future. When was that?

Touch dot B. That dot shows the year that Thrig was from. What year was that?

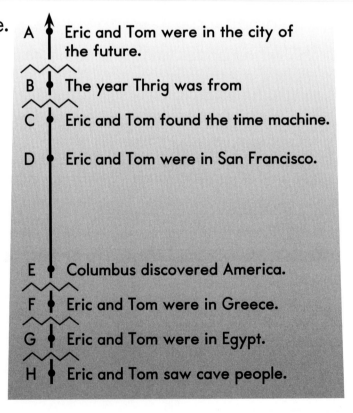

A — Eric and Tom were in the city of the future.

B — The year Thrig was from

C — Eric and Tom found the time machine.

D — Eric and Tom were in San Francisco.

E — Columbus discovered America.

F — Eric and Tom were in Greece.

G — Eric and Tom were in Egypt.

H — Eric and Tom saw cave people.

Touch dot D. That dot shows when Eric and Tom were in San Francisco. What year was that?

Touch dot E. That dot shows when Columbus discovered America. What year was that?

Touch dot F. That dot shows when Eric and Tom were in Greece. How long ago was that?

Touch dot G. That dot shows when Eric and Tom were in Egypt. How long ago was that?

Touch dot H. That dot shows when Eric and Tom saw the cave people. How long ago was that?

C The Dog and the Time Machine

Tom and Eric ran up the hill to the time machine. Tom looked inside. The big white dog was crouched down near the handle.

"Grrrrrr," the dog said, and Tom could see his teeth. The dog was very dirty and very skinny.

Eric looked inside and then whispered, "Tom, he's right next to the handle. If he bumps into that handle, the machine might disappear and we'll never get back home."

The fat man pushed past Tom and Eric. He was holding a big stick. "Let me at that dog," the man said. "I will give him a beating he will remember."

"No," Tom said and grabbed the man's arm. "Don't scare him."

The man looked at the inside of the time machine. He

looked at the dials. He watched the lights go on and off. Suddenly, he looked very frightened. "I have never seen such a thing as this machine," he said softly.

Tom hardly heard what the man said. Tom held out his hand. "Come here, boy," he said very softly.

"Grrrrrr," the dog said and showed his teeth again.

Tom turned to the man. "Do you have some food we can give the dog?" Tom asked.

"No, no," the man said. "I do not want to be around that dog or that machine." The man started to run back down the hill.

Eric said, "That dog doesn't like you, Tom. Let me talk to him."

Tom stepped out of the doorway. Eric went inside and moved toward the dog very slowly. The dog crouched lower and lower as Eric moved toward him. "Don't be afraid of me," Eric said softly.

The dog did not show his teeth. Slowly, Eric reached out and patted the dog on his head. The dog's tail wagged a little. Eric said, "You are a very nice dog."

Eric backed away ⭐ from the dog. "Come here," he said softly.

The dog stood up. His back was only about a centimeter from the handle. Tom could hardly watch. "Come here," Eric said again.

The dog took another step. Then he wagged his tail. His tail banged against the handle. "Oh, no," Tom said to himself.

But the dog's tail did not move the handle. The dog walked up to Eric. The dog jumped up on Eric and licked his face. "Tom, he likes me," Eric said.

Tom patted the dog's head. Then Tom looked outside the time machine. The fat man was near his shack, talking to three soldiers. The fat man pointed toward the time machine.

Tom said, "We'd better get out of here. Take the dog outside."

"No," Eric said. "Those men might hurt him. We've got to take him with us."

The soldiers started running up the hill. Tom ran over to the seat and sat down. Swwwwwssssssh—the door closed.

A few moments later, a soldier was yelling and banging on the door. BOOM, BOOM.

Eric said, "Hurry up, Tom, before he breaks the door."

BOOM, BOOM, BOOM.

Tom grabbed the handle and pulled on it. It didn't move. The dog was crouched in front of the door. "Grrrrrr," the dog growled. Tom pulled on the handle. The handle moved.

The dials clicked and buzzed. The dog let out a little yelp. Then, as the force died down, the dog sniffed the air.

Eric said, "Tom, you pulled down on the handle. You should have pushed up."

Tom stood up and the door opened. The dog jumped back. The time machine was on another hill above water. And there was a ship down below them near the shore. The air outside was cool.

Tom pointed to the ship. "That is a Viking ship."

The Viking ship moved slowly along the shore of the ocean.

MORE NEXT TIME

D Number your paper from 1 through 23.

Story Items

Tell about the dog that Tom and Eric found in Spain.

1. Write one word that tells how fat the dog was.

2. Write one word that tells about the color of the dog.

3. Write one word that tells about the size of the dog.

small	large	middle-sized	white
black	spotted	fat	skinny

Skill Items

The army was soundly defeated near the village.

4. What word means **beaten?**

5. What word means **small town?**

6. What word means **completely** or **really?**

Review Items

7. **Write the letters** of the 4 places that are in the United States.

a. Turkey   e. Chicago   h. Denver

b. China   f. Ohio   i. Alaska

c. Mexico   g. Japan   j. Canada

d. Italy

8. Which picture shows the smallest force?

9. Which picture shows the largest force?

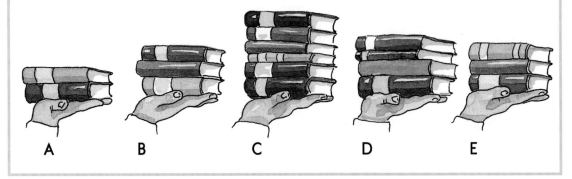

A   B   C   D   E

10. Write the letters of the 3 places that are in North America.

a. Mexico   d. Canada   f. Spain
b. Italy   e. Japan   g. United States
c. China

11. Let's say you saw a ship far out on the ocean. Would you be able to see the **whole ship** or just the **top part?**

12. Would you see **more** of the ship or **less** of the ship if the world was flat?

13. What is it called when the sun comes up?
    • sunset   • sunrise

14. What is it called when the sun goes down?
    • sunset   • sunrise

15. Who discovered America?

16. When did he discover America?

17. Is the world **round** or **flat?**

18. Did Columbus think that the world was **round** or **flat?**

19. Which letter shows Italy?

20. Which letter shows Egypt?

21. Which letter shows the Nile River?

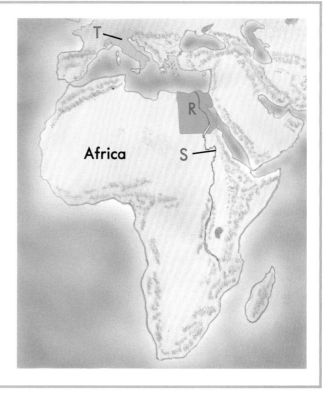

22. In what year did Eric fall into a crack in the earth?

23. A mile is a little more than ▮▮▮▮ feet.

A

1
1. wrestle
2. helmet
3. voices
4. fighters
5. village
6. probably

B

Vikings

In today's story you will read about Vikings. Here are some facts about Vikings:
- Vikings were great fighters.
- Vikings sailed across the ocean to America before Columbus did.

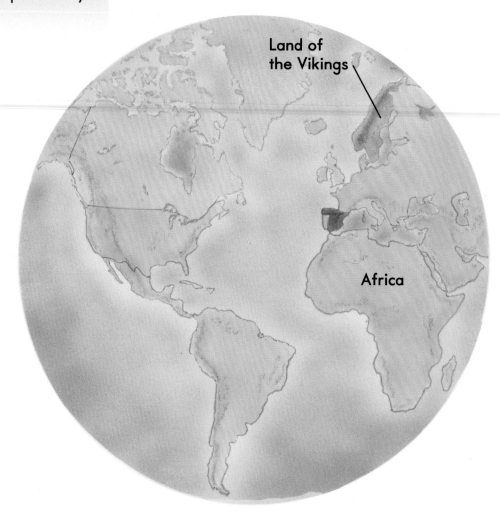

Land of the Vikings

Africa

- Vikings lived far north of Italy and Spain. The map shows where the Vikings lived.
- The Vikings lived where the winters are very long and cold.

C   The Land of the Vikings

Tom and Eric were standing on the top of a hill looking at a Viking ship on the ocean below them. Tom figured that he and Eric were probably close to the year 1000. The Viking ship was moving slowly along the shore. Tom could hear the voices of the men on the ship as they sang. But he could not understand the words of the song.

As Tom watched the Viking ship, it turned and went out to sea. Eric asked, "Didn't the Vikings go to America before Columbus did?"

Tom said, "The Vikings sailed to America long before Columbus did." Suddenly, the dog turned around and started to growl. Tom turned around. A very big man was behind them. The man was dressed in a robe made of animal skins. He wore a helmet with horns on either side.

"Grrrr," the dog growled.

The Viking looked at the dog and smiled. "Nur su urf," he said.

Tom said, "We can't understand your language."

The Viking pointed to the dog and smiled again. "Su urf," he said.

Eric said, "I think he's trying to tell us that he likes our dog."

The Viking touched Tom's shirt. "Su urf," he said. Then he pointed to the time machine. Again he said, "Su urf."

Eric said, "I think he likes everything, Tom."

The Viking waved his hand and then pointed. "Ul fas e mern," he said.

"He wants us to come with him," Eric said.

So Tom, Eric, and the dog followed the Viking into a grove of trees. They walked down a hill on the other side of the grove. At last they came to a little village. There were many huts and many dogs. The dogs started to bark.

The white dog growled at the other dogs.

People came from their huts and looked at Tom and Eric. The Viking who was walking with them told the people something and the people smiled.

A big gray dog came up to Eric and Tom's dog. Suddenly, the dogs started to fight and the Vikings started to cheer. Eric said, "Tom, stop them."

Tom moved toward the dogs, but a Viking grabbed his arm and shook his head. "In sing e tool," he said.

The dogs continued to fight. The gray dog was as big as

the white dog, and he looked stronger than the white dog. But the white dog was a little faster. Again and again the gray dog jumped at the white dog, but the white dog got out of the way. Both dogs became tired. The white dog had a cut on his neck. The gray dog's leg was hurt. Suddenly, the gray dog stopped fighting. He was about a yard from the white dog. He crouched down. The white dog started to move toward him, and the gray dog turned away.

All the people cheered. A woman ran over to the white dog. He growled at her, and everybody cheered again. Then she gave him a great big bone.

Tom said, "I think our dog just beat their best dog."

Three Vikings came over and patted Tom and Eric on the back. They led Tom and Eric to a large building. It was very dark inside the building. There were no windows, but there were many dogs and many tables. And it smelled bad.

The Vikings sat down at one of the tables. Tom and Eric sat next to them. Then some Viking women brought in great pieces of cooked meat. Each Viking took his knife and cut off a big piece. One of the Vikings cut pieces for Tom and Eric.

Eric said, "How are we supposed to eat? We don't have any forks."

Tom pointed to the Vikings. "Just eat the way they are eating." The Vikings were eating with their hands.

Suddenly, the dogs outside began to bark again. All the Vikings stopped eating. A boy ran into the building. "Left ingra," he yelled. The Vikings grabbed their knives and ran out of the building.

MORE NEXT TIME

D Number your paper from 1 through 23.

1. Which letter shows where the Land of the Vikings is?
2. Which letter shows where Italy is?
3. Which letter shows where Spain is?
4. Which letter shows where Greece is?
5. Which letter shows where Turkey is?
6. Which letter shows where Egypt is?
7. Which letter shows where San Francisco is?

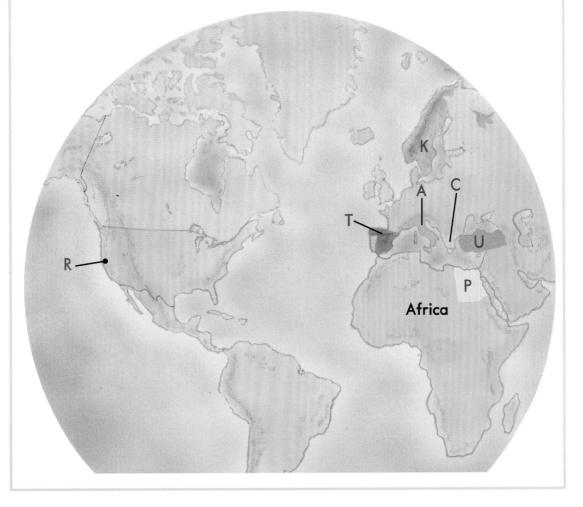

8. Who sailed across the ocean first, the Vikings or Columbus?

9. Copy 2 words that tell what the winters were like where the Vikings lived.
   - short   • cool   • cold   • long   • sunny

Skill Items

Use the words in the box to write complete sentences.

probably	defeated	attacked	appliance	argument
village	valley	convinced	soundly	studied

10. His ▮▮▮▮ ▮▮▮▮ them to buy an ▮▮▮▮.

11. The army was ▮▮▮▮ ▮▮▮▮ near the ▮▮▮▮.

Write the word from the box that means the same thing as the underlined part of each sentence.

lowered	future	jungle	buried
survived	blade	tumbled	

12. The clothes <u>turned over and over</u> in the dryer.

13. Many strange plants live in the <u>warm, wet forest</u>.

14. Our dog <u>lived through</u> her illness.

Review Items

15. Where did the time machine take Eric and Tom after they left Egypt?
    • Greece   • San Francisco   • City of the Future
16. What was the teacher in the story wearing?

17. During the war between part of Greece and Troy, what kept the soldiers from getting inside Troy?
18. At last, the Greek army built a ▪▪▪▪.
19. What was inside this object?
20. What did the men do at night?

21. How far back in time were Eric and Tom when they saw animals that no longer live on earth?
    • 40 thousand years in the future
    • 4 thousand years ago   • 40 thousand years ago

22. **Write the letters** of 3 animals the boys saw 40 thousand years ago.
    a. saber-toothed tiger   e. alligator
    b. bear   f. pig
    c. lion   g. cow
    d. horse   h. mammoth

23. When did Columbus discover America?

1

1. snowing
2. attacked
3. flakes
4. marching

2

1. wrestle
2. church
3. beard
4. outside
5. puzzle

B

More About Time

Look at the time line. Touch dot C. That dot shows when Eric and Tom started their trip. What year was that?

Touch dot A. That dot shows when Eric and Tom were in the city of the future. When was that?

Touch dot B. That dot shows the year that Thrig was from. What year was that?

Touch dot D. That dot shows when Eric and Tom were in San Francisco. What year was that?

Touch dot E. That dot shows when Columbus discovered America. What year was that?

Touch dot F. That dot shows when Eric and Tom were in the Land of the Vikings. What year was that?

Touch dot G. That dot shows when Eric and Tom were in Greece. How long ago was that?

Touch dot H. That dot shows when Eric and Tom were in Egypt. How long ago was that?

Touch dot I. That dot shows when Eric and Tom saw the cave people. How long ago was that?

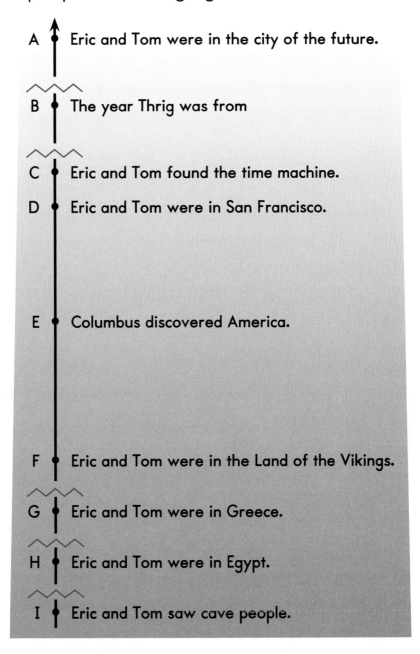

A ● Eric and Tom were in the city of the future.

B ● The year Thrig was from

C ● Eric and Tom found the time machine.

D ● Eric and Tom were in San Francisco.

E ● Columbus discovered America.

F ● Eric and Tom were in the Land of the Vikings.

G ● Eric and Tom were in Greece.

H ● Eric and Tom were in Egypt.

I ● Eric and Tom saw cave people.

C Trying to Get Home

Tom and Eric were inside the dark Viking building. Suddenly, the Vikings were fighting outside. The Vikings were using big, heavy swords and knives. Vikings from another village had attacked. These Vikings wore bands around their arms. Their leader was a huge man with a red beard.

Tom said, "I've got an idea." He started his tape recorder and ran outside. "Stop fighting! I am the god of sounds!" he yelled.

A Viking looked at him. "Un sur" he yelled.

Tom quickly played back the tape.

Some of the Vikings stopped fighting. They looked at Tom. Now more Vikings stopped fighting. Tom played the recording again and again. Soon all of the Vikings were looking at Tom.

One Viking raised his sword. His voice boomed out, "Esen trala."

Tom played back the Viking's voice: "Esen trala."

The Viking dropped his sword and stared at Tom. Then he turned to some of the other Vikings and said, "Su urf." The Vikings smiled. Then they started to laugh. They laughed and laughed. Some of them laughed so hard they almost fell over. The leader of the Vikings came over and grabbed Tom. He lifted Tom high into the air. All the Vikings held up their swords. "Sorta groob!" they shouted. "Sorta groob!"

The Vikings carried Eric and Tom into the dark building. All the Vikings sat down—the Vikings from both villages. There was shouting and yelling and dogs barking. Everybody ate and drank. For a long time, the Vikings sang and the dogs barked.

Then the Vikings went outside. Two Vikings started to wrestle. The other Vikings cheered, and the dogs barked. The two great Vikings rolled over and over on the ground.

Finally, the smaller Viking won. All the Vikings cheered. The Viking who lost stood up, smiled, and put one arm around the neck of the other Viking.

Later in the evening, Tom, Eric, and the dog walked back to the time machine. The Vikings followed. They sang.

Some of the Vikings looked inside ⭐ the time machine. Then Tom motioned so that the Vikings would move away from the time machine. Tom sat down in the seat. The door closed.

Eric said, "Let's try to get to our year. I'm tired of going through time."

Tom pushed up on the handle. Dials started to click. Lights went on and off. Tom felt the force push against his ears. Then the force died down.

Tom stood up. The door opened. A blast of cold air came into the time machine. Outside it was snowing. The snow started to blow into the time machine.

Eric said, "Tom, let's get out of here. It's too cold out there."

Tom said, "How are we going to know where we are if we don't go outside and look around?"

Eric said, "But Tom, we'll freeze out there."

The time machine was on the top of a hill. The snow was coming down so hard that Tom could not see very far. He could see a grove of trees in the distance, but he couldn't see beyond.

Tom said, "I'll run to the grove and take a look. Maybe I can find somebody who can tell us the date. I'll be right back."

Tom ran from the time machine. He ran through the snow. It was deep and cold. His shoes filled up with snow. The cold wind cut through his shirt. Tom ran to the trees and looked into the distance. He didn't see anything.

But then Tom heard something. It sounded like a bell, very far away. So he ran through the trees toward the sound of the bell. He still couldn't see anything. And he was getting very cold. "I'd better get back to the time machine," he said to himself. He started to run back. The snow was coming down much harder now. Big fluffy flakes filled the air.

Tom ran back through the trees. Then he stopped and looked. He could not see the time machine. He called out, "Eric!" Then he listened. No answer. Tom was lost. The cold was cutting into his fingers and ears.

MORE NEXT TIME

D Number your paper from 1 through 19.

Story Items

Here are some things the Vikings said:
    a. Su urf.   b. Ul fas e mern.   c. Left ingra.
1. Write the letter of the words that mean **I like that.**
2. Write the letter of the words that mean **Danger, danger.**
3. Write the letter of the words that mean **come with me.**

4. Why did the Vikings like Tom and Eric's dog?

Skill Items

5. Compare object A and object B. Remember, first tell how they're the same. Then tell how they're different.

Object A   Object B

Review Items

6. Which arrow shows the way the air will leave the jet engines?

7. Which arrow shows the way the jet will move?

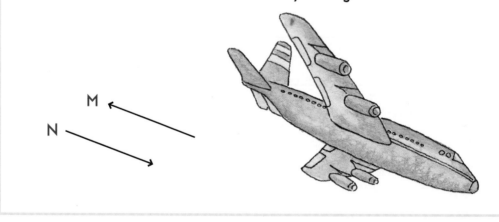

8. When a person makes an object for the first time, the person ▆▆▆▆ the object.

9. Which letter shows where Italy is?
10. Which letter shows where Egypt is?
11. Which letter shows where Greece is?
12. Which letter shows where Turkey is?
13. Which letter shows where Spain is?
14. Which letter shows where the Land of the Vikings is?

15. Who sailed across the ocean first, the Vikings or Columbus?

16. Write the letters of the 5 names that tell about time.
17. Write the letter of the one name that tells about temperature.
18. Write the letters of the 6 names that tell about distance or length.
19. Write the letters of the 2 names that tell about speed.

a. minutes   f. miles   k. hours
b. centimeters   g. degrees   l. meters
c. years   h. weeks   m. feet per minute
d. inches   i. feet   n. days
e. yards   j. miles per hour

SPECIAL PROJECT

A story that tells about a real person and that reports things that are true is called a **biography.** You may be able to find biographies of several Vikings. One is Leif Ericson; another is Eric the Red.

Look for a biography about one of these men and write three important things about his life.

A

1
1. August
2. character
3. microphone
4. valley
5. puzzled

2
1. <u>marching</u>
2. <u>president</u>
3. <u>Robert</u>
4. <u>fireplace</u>
5. <u>Concord</u>

3
1. wrapped
2. dying
3. losing
4. studied
5. shooting

4
1. George Washington
2. spy
3. lad
4. church

B ## Facts About the United States

Here are facts about things that happened when the United States became a country:

- The United States had been part of another country called England.
- In 1776, the United States announced that it was a new country.

- England said the United States could not be a new country and went to war with the United States.
- The leader of the United States Army was George Washington.
- The United States won the war with England.
- George Washington became the first president of the United States.

C Concord

"I must keep moving," Tom said to himself. He was afraid. He started running through the deep snow. He could see his breath, but no footprints. The snow had almost stopped. The cold air cut through his shirt. He ran and he ran.

Suddenly, he stopped. In a valley below there was a little village. There was a horse and rider moving slowly down the street. A few people were standing in front of a church. The church bell was ringing—"gong, gong, gong." The village looked very peaceful.

Tom ran down the hill and into the village. Tom ran toward the people who were standing in front of the church. A man said, "You should be wearing a coat."

Tom said, "I'm . . . lost."

Another man said, "Come inside, lad."

The men took Tom into the church. Tom sat down near a fireplace. The heat felt good. Tom rubbed his hands together. Slowly, the cold feeling in his hands and feet started to go away.

Tom turned to one of the men and said, "What year is it?"

The man smiled. "Everyone knows what year this is. This is 1777."

Tom said to himself, "1777." Then he asked, "And where am I?"

"You are in the town of Concord."

Tom thought for a moment. The United States became a country in 1776. It was a year later now, and the United States was at war with England. The United States was losing the war.

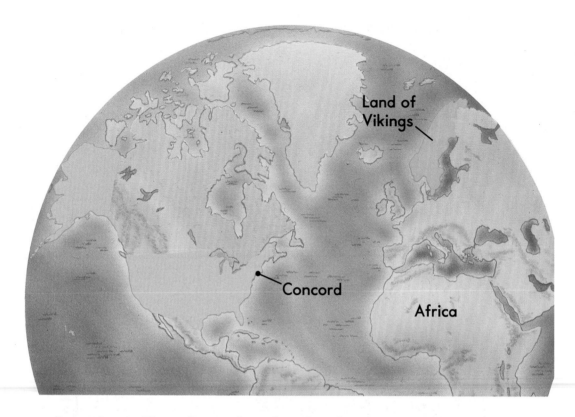

Land of Vikings

Concord

Africa

Just then, Tom heard a dog barking outside the church. The white dog was standing in the middle of the street. Tom ran up to the dog. "Where's Eric?" Tom asked.

🌸 The dog barked and ran down the street. Tom started to run after him. A man caught up to Tom and said, "Here." He handed Tom a big coat. It was made of fur. Tom ⭐ put it on as he ran. The coat was very warm. The man who ran with Tom was tall and skinny. He took great big steps, and Tom had trouble keeping up with him.

"My name is Robert," the man said as they ran along.

They followed the dog up a hill and down the other side. Then they saw Eric. He was sitting in 🌸 the snow, crying. He looked very cold. Robert took off his coat and wrapped it around Eric. Eric said, "I . . . I got lost." The dog licked his face. Eric patted the dog on the head.

Eric, Tom, and Robert started walking back to town. Eric studied Robert's clothes and said, "We are not in the right year, are we?"

Tom said to Eric, "I'll tell you about the year we're in. Right now, George Washington and his army are sick and hungry. Many of them are dying."

Robert said, "And Washington will not be able to make it through the winter. The English are going to win the war."

"No," Tom said. "The United States will win."

Robert laughed. "You talk like a fool. Some of Washington's men don't have shoes. They don't have food. How can they win a battle?"

Just as Tom was going to answer Robert's question, he noticed the town below them. He could see English soldiers marching into the town. They wore red coats. Robert said, "The English are looking for spies. If they find a spy, they shoot him."

Just then a shot sounded through the hills. One of the English soldiers dropped to the snow. Another shot sounded. The soldiers ran this way and that way.

Robert said, "Some of Washington's men are shooting at the English."

"Kazinnnnng." Something hit a tree next to Eric. Tom said, "Hey, the English are shooting at us."

"Zuuuuuuump." Another shot hit the snow near Tom. Tom yelled, "Let's get out of here."

MORE NEXT TIME

D Number your paper from 1 through 22.

Story Items

1. Which letter shows where San Francisco is?
2. Which letter shows where Egypt is?
3. Which letter shows where Greece is?
4. Which letter shows where the Land of the Vikings is?
5. Which letter shows where Concord is?
6. Which letter shows where Spain is?

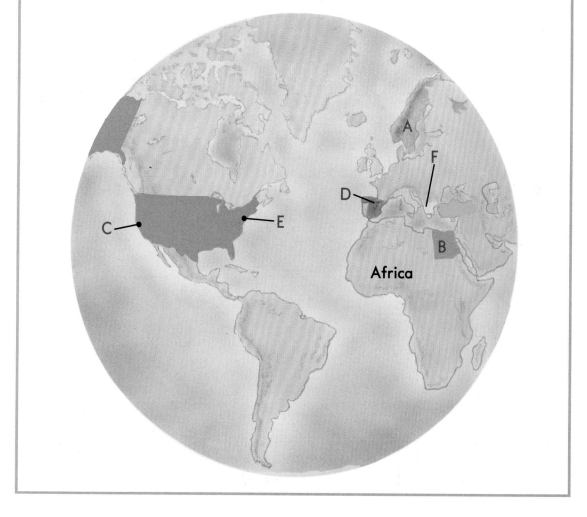

Review Items

7. How many legs does an insect have?

8. How many legs does a fly have?

9. How many legs does a bee have?

10. How many legs does a spider have?

11. How many parts does a fly's body have?

12. How many parts does a spider's body have?

13. In Egypt, Eric and Tom saw some huge stones on rafts. What were the stones for?

14. Why didn't the people in Egypt use trucks to haul things?

15. Write the letters that tell about a mammoth.
    a. long hair   c. short hair
    b. long tusks   d. short tusks

16. Write the letters that tell about an elephant of today.
    a. long hair   c. short hair
    b. long tusks   d. short tusks

17. Write the letters that tell about a saber-toothed tiger.
    a. long teeth   c. no teeth   e. no ears
    b. short tail   d. long tail   f. short teeth

18. Write the letters that tell about a tiger of today.
    a. long teeth   c. no teeth   e. no ears
    b. short tail   d. long tail   f. short teeth

19. When did Columbus discover America?

20. In what year did the United States become a country?

21. Let's say you saw a ship far out on the ocean. Would you be able to see the **whole ship** or just the **top part?**

22. Would you see **more** of the ship or **less** of the ship if the world was flat?

SPECIAL PROJECT

You have learned what a biography is. There are biographies of George Washington.

Find a biography about George Washington and write three important things about his life. Don't write about anything that you've already read about in your textbook.

A

1
1. puzzled
2. creaked
3. cracked
4. August

2
1. described
2. dashboard
3. microphone
4. voice
5. character

B   **More About** Time

Look at the time line. Touch dot C. That dot shows when Eric and Tom started their trip. What year was that?

Touch dot A. That dot shows when Eric and Tom were in the city of the future. When was that?

Touch dot B. That dot shows the year that Thrig was from. What year was that?

Touch dot D. That dot shows when Eric and Tom were in San Francisco. What year was that?

Touch dot E. That dot shows when Eric and Tom were in Concord. What year was that?

Touch dot F. That dot shows when the United States became a country. What year was that?

Touch dot G. That dot shows when Columbus discovered America. What year was that?

Touch dot H. That dot shows when Eric and Tom were in the Land of the Vikings. What year was that?

Touch dot I. That dot shows when Eric and Tom were in Greece. How long ago was that?

Touch dot J. That dot shows when Eric and Tom were in Egypt. How long ago was that?

Touch dot K. That dot shows when Eric and Tom saw the cave people. How long ago was that?

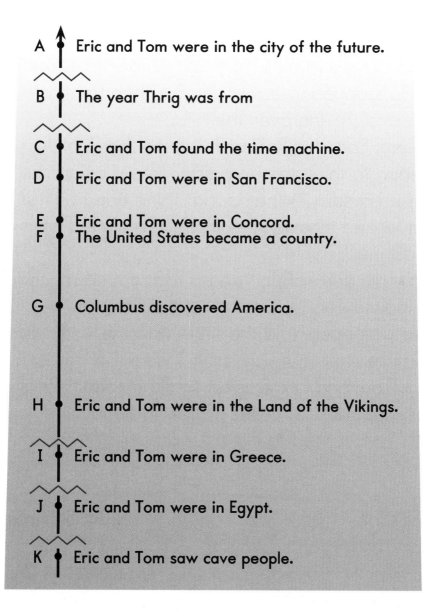

A Eric and Tom were in the city of the future.

B The year Thrig was from

C Eric and Tom found the time machine.
D Eric and Tom were in San Francisco.

E Eric and Tom were in Concord.
F The United States became a country.

G Columbus discovered America.

H Eric and Tom were in the Land of the Vikings.

I Eric and Tom were in Greece.

J Eric and Tom were in Egypt.

K Eric and Tom saw cave people.

C Home

Tom, Eric, and Robert were running from the English soldiers. After they ran about a mile, Tom stopped and said, "We don't know where we're going." He turned around. "But the dog knows." Tom bent down next to the dog. "Take us back to the time machine," Tom said.

Tom gave the dog a little push. The dog sniffed the air and then started to run. He stopped to sniff some animal tracks. He stopped to eat snow. But then he started to run in a straight line over the hills.

So Tom, Eric, and Robert followed the dog. Just when Tom began to think the dog didn't know where he was going, Robert said, "What is that thing ahead of us?"

Tom looked through the trees. "That's it. That's our time machine."

Tom, Eric, and Robert ran up to the time machine. Robert looked very puzzled. The door to the time machine was open, and the time machine was filled with snow. There was so much snow inside that the seat was covered. Tom and Eric started to dig through the snow. They pushed most of it out of the time machine.

Then Tom turned to Robert. Tom said, "You'd better come with us. If the English soldiers find you, they'll kill you."

"No," Robert said. "I am going to fight the English. I will join Washington's army."

Eric took off Robert's coat and handed it to him. "You will need this," he said.

Tom took off his coat. He said, "And you can give this to one of the other soldiers."

Robert took the coats. He put one on and threw the other over his shoulder. "Good luck," he said.

Robert started running down the hill. Soon he had disappeared into the woods. Three soldiers in red coats were coming from the other direction.

Tom sat down in the seat. The door did not close. Tom said, "The seat must be frozen." He bounced up and down. The English soldiers were very close. The dog was standing in the doorway growling at them. One soldier came up to the doorway. "Come out of there," he yelled.

Eric pushed on the seat. Tom bounced up and down. Suddenly, the seat creaked and—swwwwsh—the door closed.

"Bong! Bong!"

"I hope the handle works," Tom said. He pulled on the handle, but it seemed to be frozen.

Tom banged on the dashboard. Suddenly, a door opened

and a microphone popped out. A voice said, "What year and month do you wish to go to?"

Eric and Tom looked at each other. "The month we want is August," Eric said. Then he told the year. The handle moved. Several dials lit up. Then the voice said, "What date in August?"

Eric said, "The 19th. It is a Saturday."

Again the end of the handle moved, and several more dials lit up. The voice said, "What time on August 19th?"

Tom said, "Make it about the time the sun goes down."

The voice said, "What place do you wish to go to on August 19th?"

Eric described the place. The voice said, "On August 19th, the sun sets at 8:32 P.M. in that place."

Eric asked Tom, "Who are we talking to?"

The voice said, "I am the computer that runs this time machine."

Suddenly, the force pushed against Tom. Then the force died down. Slowly, Tom stood up and the boys went outside.

The time machine was on the mountain where Tom and Eric had found it. Thrig was standing next to the time machine. He told the boys, "I feel better now. I think I can make the trip back to the year 2400." He got in the time machine. The door closed, and a moment later, the time machine disappeared. Eric said, "I hope he makes it."

Tom said, "Me, too." Then he looked down the mountain and could see the other kids walking home down the path below.

"Let's get out of here," Tom said. Tom yelled out to the other kids, "Hey wait for us!"

Tom, Eric, and the dog caught up to the other kids. Someone asked, "Hey, where did you get the dog?"

Tom smiled. "You wouldn't believe me if I told you."

Another kid asked, "What's the dog's name?"

Eric said, "Columbus."

"That's a silly name for a dog," one kid said.

Eric said, "It's not a silly name for <u>this</u> dog."

One of the girls said, "Let's go home. We've got a long way to go."

Tom laughed. "We don't have very far to go at all." Eric laughed too.

"Wow!" Tom said. "It sure feels good to be home." He patted Columbus on the head. Columbus wagged his tail. The lights were going on all over the town below. That town sure looked good.

THE END

D Number your paper from 1 through 20.

Review Items

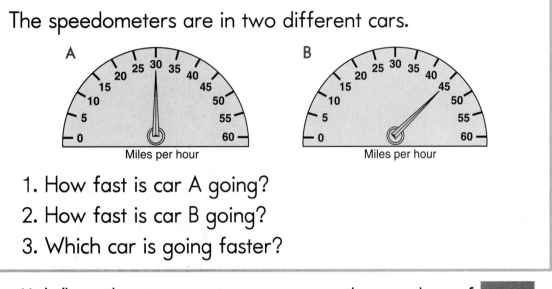

The speedometers are in two different cars.

A   Miles per hour

B   Miles per hour

1. How fast is car A going?
2. How fast is car B going?
3. Which car is going faster?

4. When the temperature goes up, the number of ▮▮▮▮ gets bigger.
    • miles   • degrees   • hours   • miles per hour

5. When the United States announced that it was a country, England went to war with the United States. Who was the leader of the United States army during the war?

6. Which country won the war?

7. Which country was winning that war in 1777?

8. Who was the first president of the United States?

9. Who is the president of the United States today?

Write the letter that shows where each place is.

10. Italy
11. Egypt
12. Greece
13. Turkey
14. Spain
15. Land of the Vikings

16. Concord
17. San Francisco
18. Canada
19. United States
20. Mexico

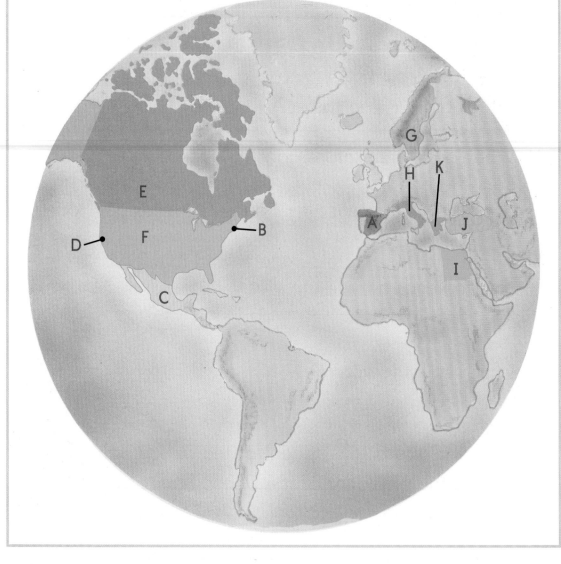

End-of-Program Test

Number your paper from 1 through 30.

1. Who sailed across the ocean first, the Vikings or Columbus?

2. When the United States announced that it was a country, England went to war with the United States. Who was the leader of the United States army during the war?

3. Which country won the war?

4. Which country was winning that war in 1777?

5. Who was the first president of the United States?

6. Who is the president of the United States today?

7. In what year did the United States become a country?

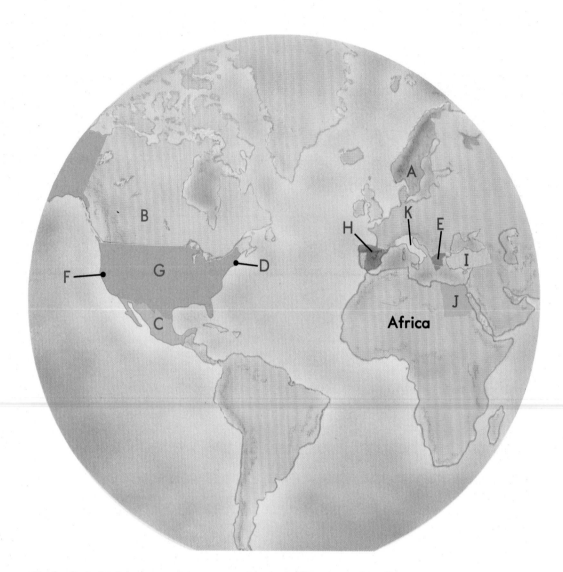

8. Which letter shows where Greece is?

9. Which letter shows where Turkey is?

10. Which letter shows where Spain is?

11. Which letter shows where the Land of Vikings is?

12. Which letter shows where Concord is?

13. Which letter shows where Canada is?

14. Which letter shows where Mexico is?

Write the time for each event shown on the time line.

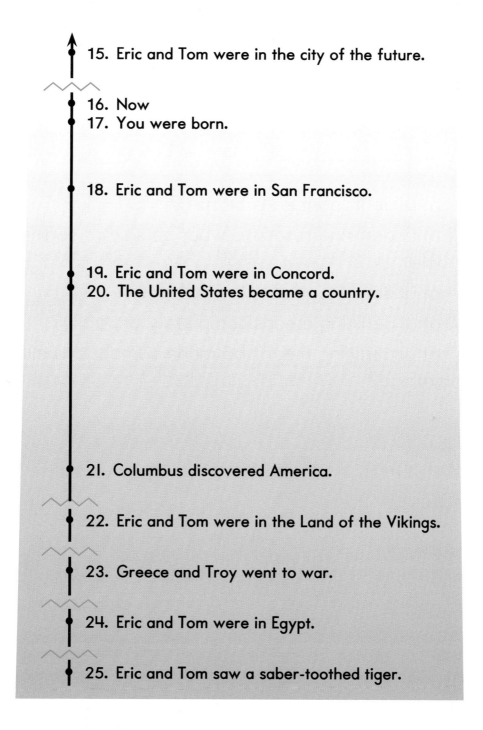

15. Eric and Tom were in the city of the future.

16. Now
17. You were born.

18. Eric and Tom were in San Francisco.

19. Eric and Tom were in Concord.
20. The United States became a country.

21. Columbus discovered America.

22. Eric and Tom were in the Land of the Vikings.

23. Greece and Troy went to war.

24. Eric and Tom were in Egypt.

25. Eric and Tom saw a saber-toothed tiger.

Skill Items

For each item, write the underlined word or words from the sentences in the box.

> The army was <u>soundly</u> <u>defeated</u> near the <u>village</u>.
> His <u>argument</u> <u>convinced</u> them to buy an <u>appliance</u>.

26. What underlining means **beaten?**
27. What underlining refers to what he said to convince people?
28. What underlining means a **small town?**
29. What underlining means **completely** or **really?**
30. What underlining means he made somebody believe something?

Special Items

1. Below is a list of some of the stories you read in this program. Write the letters of your **2 favorite** stories.
   a. Tina the apple tree saves the forest.
   b. Joe Williams gets a new job.
   c. Aunt Fanny learns how to share.
   d. Goad the toad escapes from the Browns.
   e. Nancy learns about being tiny.
   f. Herman the fly flies around the world.
   g. Linda and Kathy survive on an island.
   h. Bertha uses her nose.
   i. Andrew Dexter learns about being super strong.
   j. Toby the kangaroo finds his father.
   k. Eric and Tom travel in a time machine.
   l. The word bank solves its problems.

2. Below is a list of some of the characters you read about in this program. Write the letters of your **3 favorite** characters.
   a. Aunt Fanny
   b. Goad the toad
   c. Nancy
   d. Herman the fly
   e. Linda
   f. Kathy
   g. Bertha Turner
   h. Maria Sanchez the investigator
   i. Achilles
   j. Andrew Dexter
   k. Toby the kangaroo
   l. Eric
   m. Tom

3. What place that you read about would you like to learn more about?

4. What did you like most about this program?

5. What did you like least about this program?

SPECIAL PROJECT

Make a time line that shows facts about your school and some of the people in it. Show the following events on your time line:

1. When the youngest student in your class was born.

2. When the oldest student in your class was born.

3. When you will enter high school.

4. When you will graduate from high school.

5. When your teacher or principal was born.

6. When your school was built.

You may want to show pictures of the people or things named on your time line. You may want to add other events that are important to your school or the students in your class.

Fact Game Answer Key

2. A – pony
   B – Mongolian horse
   C – quarter horse

3. a. earlier
   b. later

4. a. B
   b. J
   c. M

5. hopped, hopper, hopping

6. walker, walks, walked

7. running, runner, ran

8. X – United States
   Y – Pacific Ocean

9. J – Italy
   K – Japan
   M – Turkey

10. Idea: The war between Greece and Troy

11. a. 1776
    b. 1903

12. a. Ask your teacher.
    b. Ask your teacher.

2. a. (over) 10 feet
   b. 3 centimeters

3. a. Idea: In its mother's pouch
   b. half a year

4. a. Canada
   b. Australia
   c. India

5. Pacific Ocean

6. A – United States
   B – Pacific Ocean

7. C – Canada
   D – Australia
   E – Alaska

8. 60

9. a. United States
   b. Canada
   c. United States

10. 5 minutes

11. a. mob
    b. joey

12. A – koala
    B – platypus
    C – kangaroo

Lesson 130

2. boxing gloves

3. homonym

4. a. M
   b. J

5. a. Chicago
   b. 1871

6. a. can not
   b. you have
   c. we are

7. right – C
   here – D
   rode – B
   four – A

8. a. houses
   b. office buildings,
      stores

9. a. Check with your
      teacher.
   b. 2400

10. a. push
    b. push

11. here

12. a. Idea: Sit in the seat.
    b. Idea: Pull the
       handle.

Lesson 140

2. 1868, 1796, 1996

3. 2100, 2010, 2222

4. yards,
   feet,
   centimeters

5. days,
   hours,
   weeks

6. inches per minute,
   meters per week,
   feet per second

7. A. 4 thousand years in
      the future
   B. 2400
   C. Check with your
      teacher.

8. D. Check with your
      teacher.
   E. 1906
   F. 1776

9. G. 3 thousand years
      ago
   H. 5 thousand years
      ago
   I. 40 thousand years
      ago

10. A. Egypt
    B. Italy
    C. Spain

11. D. Turkey
    E. Greece

12. Texas, New York City,
    Concord

1. You measure your weight in pounds.

2. They waded into the stream to remove tadpoles.

3. The fly boasted about escaping from the spider.

4. The workers propped up the cage with steel bars.

5. Hunters were stationed at opposite ends of the field.

6. He motioned to the flight attendant ahead of him.

7. The traffic was moving forty miles per hour.

8. He is supposed to make a decision in a couple of days.

9. Several paths continued for a great distance.

10. Boiling water will thaw ice in a few moments.

11. They were eager to hear the announcement.

12. The lifeboat disappeared in the whirlpool.

13. The smoke swirled in enormous billows.

14. The occasional foul smell was normal.

15. They constructed an enormous machine.

16. She survived until she was rescued.

17. The soldiers protected their equipment.

18. Lawyers with talent normally succeed.

19. A dozen typists approached the stairs.

20. The job required a consultant.

21. The adults huddled around the fire.

22. The customer bought a valuable gift.

23. They had reasons for interrupting her talk.

24. He frequently argued about the championship.

25. She commented about the still water.

26. Their amazing effort surprised the neighbors.

27. Police officers checked the ship's cargo.

28. The champions performed perfectly.

29. She paid the correct amount.

30. Perhaps they will reply in a few days.

31. The palace guards spoke different languages.

32. His argument convinced them to buy an appliance.

33. The army was soundly defeated near the village.

Glossary

adults   *Adults* are grown-ups.

adventure   When you have an *adventure,* you do something very exciting.

ahead   *Ahead* is another word for *in front.*

Alaska   *Alaska* is the largest state.

allow   When you *allow* somebody to do something, you permit that person to do it.

although   In some sentences, *although* is another word for *but.*

amazing   Something that is *amazing* is very hard to believe.

America   *America* is a large part of the world.

amount   The *amount* of something tells how much there is.

ancient   Things that are *ancient* are very, very old.

animal preserve   An *animal preserve* is a place that protects animals.

ankles   Your *ankles* are the joints right above your feet.

announce   When you *announce* something, you let others know about it.

announcement   An *announcement* is a message.

apart   Things that are not close to each other are far *apart.*

appear   When something first comes into sight, it *appears.*

appliances   *Appliances* are machines that are used around the house.

approach   When you *approach* something, you move toward it.

argue   When you *argue* with someone, you tell why you don't agree with what that person says.

argument   An *argument* is what you say to make people believe you.

army   An *army* is the group of people that goes to war for a country.

arrange   When things are *arranged,* the things are in place.

ashamed   When you feel *ashamed,* you feel that you've done something bad.

ashes   The stuff that is left over after something burns up is called *ashes.*

at bat   When a person is *at bat* in a baseball game, that person has a turn at hitting the ball.

attach   Something that is *attached* is connected.

attack   When people *attack,* they do something to start a fight or a battle.

attention   When something catches your *attention,* you know it's there.

Australia   *Australia* is the name of a country.

awful   Something that is *awful* is very bad.

battered   When something is *battered,* it is beaten up.

battle   A *battle* in a war is one of the smaller fights that takes place in the war.

before long   If something happens very soon, it happens *before long.*

behave   The way you *behave* is the way you act.

beyond a doubt   When you know something *beyond a doubt,* you know it for sure.

billows   *Billows* are large clouds or waves that are swelling up.

binoculars   *Binoculars* are powerful glasses that make far-off things look close.

blade   The *blade* is the flat part of a tool that is connected to a handle.

blame   When you say that things went wrong because of somebody else, you *blame* that person.

block   When you *block* in a football game, you push a player from the other team without using your hands to grab the player.

boast   *Boast* is another word for *brag.*

boil   When water *boils,* it makes lots of bubbles and steam. Water boils at 212 degrees.

boiled   Things that are *boiled* are cooked in bubbling hot water.

booms   When a voice *booms,* it's very loud.

bow   (rhymes with *how*) The *bow* is the front of a ship.

bow   (rhymes with *how*) When you *bow,* you bend forward.

broiled   Things that are *broiled* are cooked over an open fire.

buried   When something is *buried,* it has things piled on top of it.

calm   When things are *calm,* they are very quiet and peaceful.

Canada   *Canada* is one of the countries of America.

captain   The *captain* of a ship or plane is the person in charge of the vehicle.

cargo   *Cargo* is what ships carry from one place to another.

catch your breath   When you *catch your breath,* you breathe very hard.

cave   A *cave* is a hole in the ground that is big enough for people or animals to go into.

center   The *center* of something is the middle of the thing.

centimeters   *Centimeters* are used to tell how long things are. There are 100 centimeters in a meter.

certain   *Certain* is another word for *sure.*

championship   A *championship* is a contest between the two best teams.

character   A *character* is a person or animal in a story.

charge   When an animal *charges,* it puts its head down and runs at something as fast as it can go.

Chicago   *Chicago* is a large city near the middle of the United States.

chilled   When you feel cold, you feel *chilled.*

China   *China* is a large country near Japan.

claim   When you *claim* something, you say it's yours.

clomping   A *clomping* sound is the sound a horse makes when it walks on a street.

clue   *Clues* are hints.

coach   A *coach* is the person who gives orders to the players on a team.

coast   The *coast* is where the land meets the ocean.

cock your head   When you *cock your head,* you tilt it.

coconuts   *Coconuts* are fruits with heavy shells.

Columbus   The name of the man who sailed across the ocean and discovered America is *Columbus.*

comfortable   When something feels *comfortable,* it feels pretty good.

comment   When you *comment* about something, you quickly tell about that thing.

complaint   A *complaint* is a statement that tells what you don't like about something.

completely   *Completely* is another word for *totally.*

computer   *Computers* are machines that you can use to work problems and play games.

Concord   *Concord* is the name of one of the first towns in the United States.

confusion   When things are very strange and mixed up, we say things are thrown into *confusion.*

constantly   Things that go on *constantly* go on all the time.

construct   When you *construct* something, you *build* it.

consultant   A *consultant* is a person who is hired for a special job.

contest   Any game or event that has winners and losers is a *contest.*

continue   If something *continues,* it keeps on going.

convince   When you *convince* people, you make them believe something.

copilot   A *copilot* is the person who works with the pilot in flying the plane.

correct   *Correct* is another word for *right.*

cottonwood   *Cottonwood* trees are large trees.

count on   When you can be sure of something, you can *count on* that thing.

couple   A *couple* of things is two things.

crate   A *crate* is a wooden box that is used to ship things.

creek   A *creek* is a small stream.

crouch   When you *crouch,* you bend close to the ground.

current   *Currents* are places where water is moving.

customer   A person who buys things at a store is a *customer* of that store.

damage   If you do *damage* to something, you break part of it or ruin it.

danger   When you're in a place where you could get hurt, you're in *danger* of getting hurt.

dates   *Dates* are small sweet fruits that grow on some palm trees.

daydream   When you *daydream,* you think of nice things that you would like to happen.

deaf   People who are *deaf* cannot hear anything.

decision   When you make a *decision* to do something, you make up your mind to do it.

defeat   *Defeated* is another word for *beaten.*

degrees   You measure temperature in *degrees.*

demand   When you *demand* an answer, you insist on it.

Denver   *Denver* is a large city about halfway between Chicago and San Francisco.

describe   When you *describe* something, you tell how it looks or how it works.

destroy   If you ruin something so it can't be fixed, you *destroy* that thing.

direct   Things that are *direct* are straight and simple.

disappear   When something *disappears,* you can't see it anymore.

discover   The person who is the first to find something is the person who *discovers* that thing.

distance   The farther apart things are, the bigger the *distance* between them.

double   *Double* means *two times as much.*

dozen   *Dozen* is another word for *twelve.*

drifts   When something *drifts,* winds or currents make it move slowly.

dull   Things that are boring are *dull.*

during   If something happens *during* the night, it happens while the night is going on.

eager   When you're *eager* for something, you are really looking forward to it.

earlier   Something that happens *earlier* happens before another thing.

earplugs   *Earplugs* are rubber things that you stick in your ears. It is hard to hear when you are wearing earplugs.

Glossary   **347**

earth   *Earth* is another name for our world.

earth   *Earth* is another word for *dirt.*

earthquake   When an *earthquake* takes place, the ground moves and shakes and splits open.

echo   When you hear an *echo,* you hear a sound that is repeated.

effort   Something that takes a lot of strength takes a lot of *effort.*

Egypt   *Egypt* is the name of a country.

electric   Things that are *electric* run on electricity, not on fuel.

electricity   *Electricity* is the power you get when you plug things into wall outlets.

encyclopedia   An *encyclopedia* is a large set of books that gives information about anything you can name.

engine   The *engine* of a vehicle is the part that makes the vehicle run.

England   *England* is a country that is almost 4 thousand miles from the United States.

English   *English* is the name of the language that people speak in England and the United States.

enormous   *Enormous* means *very, very large.*

eohippus   *Eohippus* is the first kind of horse that lived on Earth.

equipment   Large machines and tools are called *equipment.*

escape   When you *escape* from something, you get away from it.

examine   When you *examine* something, you look at it closely.

except   *Except* is another word for *but* in some sentences.

excitement   When you are worked up and have trouble sitting still, you feel *excitement.*

exit   When you *exit* a place, you leave the place.

expensive   Things that cost a lot of money are *expensive.*

explain   When you *explain* something, you give information about that thing.

expression The *expression* on your face shows what you're feeling.

facts Sentences that give you information are *facts.*

fades When something *fades,* it slowly disappears.

fail The opposite of *succeed* is *fail.*

faint When you *faint,* you pass out.

famous If something is *famous,* it is *well-known.*

fancy If an office is *fancy,* it is not plain.

fear If you *fear* something, you are afraid of it.

field goal A *field goal* is a score in football that is made by kicking the ball.

figure out When you *figure out* something, you learn it.

finally *Finally* means *at last.*

finest Something that is the *finest* is the most expensive or the best.

fire dies down When a *fire dies down,* it doesn't go out.

fired When you are *fired* from a job, you are told you can't work at that job anymore.

first base *First base* is the first base you run to after you hit the ball in a game of baseball.

flight attendant A *flight attendant* is somebody who works on a plane and takes care of passengers.

force A *force* is a *push.*

forever If something lasts *forever,* it never never ends.

foul *Foul* is another word for bad.

frequently *Frequently* is another word for *often.*

frisky *Frisky* means *playful* or *full of energy.*

fronds *Fronds* are the branches of palm trees.

frost *Frost* is frozen water that forms on grass during cold nights.

fuel *Fuel* is what engines burn when they run.

gain When a ball carrier goes the right way in football, he makes a *gain.* When he gets tackled before he can make a gain, he makes a loss.

galley The *galley* is the kitchen on a plane or ship.

garden A *garden* is a place where you grow flowers or vegetables.

gift A *gift* is another way of saying a *present.*

globe A small model of Earth is called a *globe.*

glows When something *glows,* it gives off light.

go out for a team When you *go out for a team,* you show the coach how good you are.

grain *Grain* is the seed of grass or cereal plants.

gram A *gram* is a very small unit of weight.

graph A *graph* is a kind of a picture that has lines or parts that show different amounts.

great *Great* is another word for *wonderful.*

Greece *Greece* is the name of a country.

groceries The food that you buy at the supermarket or grocery store is called *groceries.*

grove A *grove* of trees is a small group of trees.

guard A *guard* is a person whose job is to protect something.

gust A *gust* of wind is a sudden wind that blows for a very short time.

half If you cut something in *half,* you get two pieces that are the same size. Each piece is half.

half-aware When you are *half-aware* of something, you are not paying much attention to it.

hallelujah People who say *"Hallelujah"* are feeling great joy.

harm *Harm* is another word for *hurt.*

hay *Hay* is dried grass that horses and cows eat.

heat When things feel hot, they give off *heat.*

herd A *herd* of animals is a group of animals that run together.

hoist When you *hoist* something, you lift it up.

holler Another word for *holler* is *yell.*

hollow Something that is *hollow* is not solid.

home run When a baseball player hits a *home run,* the player hits the ball so far that nobody can get it before the player runs around all four bases.

homonym A *homonym* is a word that sounds the same as another word.

honest Here's another way of saying I'm telling the truth: *honest.*

hooves *Hooves* are the kind of feet that deer and horses and cows have. *Hoof* tells about one foot. *Hooves* tells about more than one foot.

huddle When people crowd close together, they *huddle.*

human A *human* is a person.

humans *Humans* are people.

illegal Things that are *illegal* are against the law.

imagining *Imagining* is a kind of thinking.

imitate When you *imitate* somebody, you do exactly what that person does.

important If something is *important,* you should pay attention to it.

impression When you have an *impression* about something, you have an idea about that thing.

in fact Here's another way of saying that something is true: *in fact.*

India *India* is a large country on the other side of the world.

insect An *insect* is a bug that has six legs.

insist When you keep telling that you want something, you *insist* on that thing.

interrupt When you *interrupt* somebody, you start talking before the other person finishes.

investigate When you *investigate* something, you try to learn the facts about that thing.

involved People who take part in a game are *involved* in the game.

Italy *Italy* is a country near Greece.

Japan *Japan* is a country that is 5 thousand miles from the United States.

jewels *Jewels* are valuable stones.

juggle When you *juggle* objects, you keep tossing the objects in the air and you make sure that at least two objects are always in the air at the same time.

jungle A *jungle* is a forest that is always warm and wet.

Kennedy Airport *Kennedy Airport* is a large airport in New York City.

koala   A *koala* is an animal that looks like a teddy bear and lives in Australia.

lad   A *lad* is a young man.

Lake Michigan   *Lake Michigan* is one of the five Great Lakes.

language   A *language* is the words that people in a country use to say things.

lawn   *Lawn* is the name for grass that is well-kept and mowed.

lawyer   *Lawyers* are people who help us when we have questions about the law.

lean   Something that *leans* does not stand straight up and down.

ledge   A *ledge* is a narrow step that is on cliffs or mountains.

let somebody down   When you *let somebody down,* that person thinks you will help and you don't help.

lifeboats   *Lifeboats* are emergency boats that are on large ships.

lighter   *Lighter* is the opposite of *heavier.*

lookout   A *lookout* is a person who looks in all directions to see if trouble is near.

loss   When a ball carrier goes the right way in football, he makes a gain. When he gets tackled before he can make a gain, he makes a *loss.*

lowered   When something is *lowered,* it is moved down.

machine   A *machine* is something that is made to help people do work.

magnet   A *magnet* is something that hangs on to things made of steel or iron.

magnetic   Things that are *magnetic* stick to a magnet.

make sense   When things don't *make sense* to you, they are not at all clear to you.

make-believe   *Make-believe* is another word for *pretend.*

manage   When you have to work hard to do something, you *manage* do to it.

mean   When you do what you *mean* to do, you do what you plan to do.

measure   When you *measure* something, you find out how long it is or how hot it is or how heavy it is or how tall it is.

mention   When you tell just a little bit about something, you *mention* that thing.

Mexico   *Mexico* is one of the countries of America.

microphone   A *microphone* is a tool that picks up sounds.

million   A *million* is a very, very large number.

million   A *million* is one thousand thousand.

modern   *Modern* is the opposite of *old-fashioned.*

moist   Things that are *moist* are slightly wet, not dripping wet.

moments   A few *moments* is not very many seconds.

motion   When you *motion* to another person, you use your hands or body to show the person what to do.

mumble   When you *mumble,* you talk to yourself so others can't understand everything you say.

mummy   One kind of *mummy* is a dead person all wrapped up in strips of cloth.

muscle   *Muscles* are the meaty parts of your body that make your body move.

myna   A *myna* is a bird.

neighbors   *Neighbors* are people who live near you or sit near you.

New York City   *New York City* is the name of one of the largest cities in the world.

normal   *Normal* is another word for *usual.*

normally   *Normally* is another word for *usually.*

object   When you argue that something is wrong, you *object* to that thing.

occasional   *Occasional* means *once in a while.*

ocean   An *ocean* is a very large body of salt water.

offer   When you *offer* something, you give someone a chance to take it.

Ohio   *Ohio* is a state between Chicago and New York.

open field   An *open field* is a place with just grass and no trees.

opposite   Hot is the *opposite* of cold.

outcome   The *outcome* of an event is the way things turn out.

Pacific Ocean The *Pacific Ocean* is the ocean that borders the west coast of the United States.

packed When things are squeezed into a small space, they are *packed.*

palace A king and queen live in a *palace.* A *palace* is a very large and fancy place.

panel A flat part that's shaped like a rectangle is called a *panel.*

passenger A *passenger* is someone who rides in a vehicle.

peacock A *peacock* is a very large bird with beautiful feathers.

peek When you sneak a quick look at something, you *peek.*

peel Another name for the skin of an orange is the *peel* of an orange.

per *Per* means *each.*

perfect Something that is *perfect* has everything just the way it should be.

perfectly If you do something *perfectly,* you don't make any mistakes.

perform When you *perform,* you put on a show.

perhaps *Perhaps* is another word for *maybe.*

permit When you *let* people do something, you *permit* them to do it.

poison If *poison* gets inside your body, it will make your body stop working and it may kill you.

police officers *Police officers* are cops.

poster A *poster* is a large picture that tells about something.

pouch A *pouch* is a small bag that holds things.

pounds *Pounds* are a unit used to measure weight.

practice Things that you *practice* are things that you do again and again.

preserve When you *preserve* something, you save it or protect it.

president The *president* of a country is the person who has the most power to run that country.

pretend When you *pretend* to do something, you make-believe.

probably If something will *probably* happen, you are pretty sure it will happen.

professional football league
A *professional football league* is a group of teams that play football.

project A *project* is a large job.

prop up When you *prop up* something, you support the thing so it will stay in place.

protect When you *protect* something, you make sure that nothing can hurt it.

prove When you *prove* something, you show that it is true.

puzzled Another word for *confused* is *puzzled.*

pyramid A *pyramid* is a type of building found in Egypt.

queen Usually, a *queen* is the wife of a king.

raft A *raft* is a flat boat.

ramp A *ramp* is a walkway that goes uphill.

raw Food that is not cooked is *raw.*

realize When you *realize* something, you suddenly understand it for the first time.

reason When you tell why you do something, you give a *reason* for doing that thing.

receive When somebody gives you something, you *receive* it.

recognize When you *recognize* something that you see or feel, you know what it is.

record Somebody who sets a *record* does something better than anybody has done before.

referee A *referee* is a person who makes decisions about how a game is played.

refund When your money is *refunded,* it is returned.

relatives Your *relatives* are people in your family.

remain *Remain* is another word for *stay.*

remove When you *remove* something, you get rid of it or take it away.

reply *Reply* is another word for *answer.*

report When you give a *report,* you give the facts.

required Things that are *required* are needed.

rescue Somebody who is *rescued* is *saved* from some kind of danger.

respond When you *respond* to someone, you answer that person.

rich If you have lots and lots of money, you are *rich.*

rip-off A *rip-off* is a bad deal.

rise *Rise* is another word for *moves up.*

roadside A *roadside* business is a business that is alongside the road.

ruin When you *ruin* something, you destroy it or do something to it so it won't work.

rule A *rule* tells you what to do.

ruler A *ruler* is a tool that you use to measure inches or centimeters.

runway A *runway* is like a large road that airplanes use when they take off.

rushing *Rushing* is another word for *moving fast.*

Russia *Russia* is the name of a very large country.

salesperson A person who sells things is a *salesperson.*

San Francisco *San Francisco* is a city on the west coast of the United States.

scales The skin of fish is covered with *scales.*

scar A *scar* is a mark left from a bad cut or burn.

screech A *screech* is a high, sharp sound.

scold When your mother *scolds* you, she lets you know what you did wrong.

seasons Each year has four *seasons:* spring, summer, fall, winter.

sense Another word for a *feeling* is a *sense.*

service People who offer a *service* do a special job.

several *Several* things are more than two things but less than many things.

shabby Something that is *shabby* is not neat and clean.

shallow *Shallow* is the opposite of *deep.*

show up When you go to a place, you *show up* at that place.

skeleton An animal's *skeleton* is all the bones of the animal's body.

slave A *slave* is a person who has very few rights.

slight Something that is *slight* is not very big.

smooth and quiet When things are *smooth and quiet,* they are very calm.

soldiers *Soldiers* are men and women in the army.

soundly *Soundly* means *completely* or *really.*

Spain *Spain* is a country that is near Italy.

sped *Sped* is another word for *went fast.*

speedometer A *speedometer* is the dial in a vehicle that shows how fast the vehicle is moving.

spices *Spices* are things that you add to food to give it a special flavor.

spoiled *Spoiled* children cry and act like babies to make people do things for them.

spy A *spy* is a person who gives important information to the enemy.

stale Food that is *stale* is old and not very good to eat.

stands The *stands* in a ball park are the seats where people sit.

stars The best players are called *stars.*

starve When people have no food to eat for a long time, they *starve.*

stationed When someone is *stationed* in a place, the person is supposed to stay in that place.

steel *Steel* is a very tough metal.

stern The *stern* is the back of a ship.

still Another word for *silent* or *peaceful* is *still.*

strange If something looks *strange,* it does not look like you think it should look.

strength Your *strength* is how strong you are.

stretch When things *stretch* out, they are very wide or very long.

striped If something is *striped,* it has stripes.

strut *Strutting* is a kind of show-off walking.

succeed When you *succeed* at something, you do it the way you planned.

sunken ship A *sunken ship* is a ship at the bottom of the ocean.

support When you *support* something, you hold it up or hold it in place.

supposed to *Supposed to* means *should.*

survive When you *survive,* you manage to stay alive.

swirl When something *swirls,* it spins around as it drifts.

swoop Things that *swoop* move in big curves.

tackle When you *tackle* players in football, you bring them down so their knees hit the ground.

tadpoles *Tadpoles* are baby toads or frogs.

takeoff When an airplane first leaves the ground, it's called the *takeoff.*

talent People with *talent* are people with special skills.

tame *Tame* is the opposite of *wild.*

temperature When you measure the *temperature* of something, you find out how hot it is.

Texas *Texas* is the second-largest state in the United States.

thaw *Thaw* means *melt.*

thought Something that you think about is a *thought.*

thousand A *thousand* is equal to ten hundreds.

time When you *time* something, you use a watch to figure out how long it takes.

ton A *ton* is two thousand pounds.

touchdown When you score a *touchdown* in football, you take the ball across the goal line.

traffic All the vehicles that are driving on a street are the *traffic.*

treasure *Treasures* are things that are worth a lot of money.

triple *Triple* means *three times as much.*

trumpeting A *trumpeting* sound is something that sounds like it comes from a musical instrument called a trumpet.

trunk The *trunk* of a tree is the main part that comes out of the ground.

tumbles When something *tumbles,* it turns over and over.

Turkey *Turkey* is a country near Egypt.

tusks The *tusks* of an animal are huge teeth that stick out of the animal's mouth.

twig A *twig* is a tiny branch.

typist *Typists* are people who type things very neatly.

uneasy When you feel nervous, you feel *uneasy.*

unfair If rules are not the same for everybody, the rules are *unfair.*

unpleasant Things that are *unpleasant* are not nice.

usually Things that *usually* happen are things that happen most of the time.

valuable Things that are worth a lot of money are *valuable.*

Viking The *Vikings* were people who lived long ago and sailed to many parts of the world.

village A *village* is a small town.

wade When you *wade,* you walk in water that is not very deep.

war A *war* is a long fight between two countries.

warn When you *warn* people, you let them know that trouble is near.

warts *Warts* are little bumps that some people have on their body. Toads have warts, too.

water strider A *water strider* is an insect that can walk on the top of water.

we'd *We'd* is a contraction for the words *we would* or *we had.*

weak *Weak* means *not strong.*

weather When you tell about the *weather,* you tell about the temperature, the wind, the clouds, and if it is raining or snowing.

weigh When you measure how many grams or pounds something is, you *weigh* it.

weight The *weight* of an object is how heavy that object is.

well A *well* is a deep hole in the ground.

weren't *Weren't* is a contraction for the words *were not.*

whirlpool The water in a *whirlpool* goes around and around as it goes down.

whole *Whole* means all of it—the whole thing.

wise Someone who is *wise* is very smart.

worth Something is *worth* the amount of money people would pay for it.

worthless Something that is *worthless* is not worth anything.

woven Things made of cloth are *woven.*

wrap When you *wrap* a package with paper, you put paper around it.

yard A *yard* tells how long things are. A yard is almost as long as a meter.

Index

Andrew
    Andy leaves the team   23–26
    Andy loses strength   3–5, 10–12, 19
    championship game   31–33, 37–41
    coach Denny   2, 23–24, 39–40
    Mean George   4–5, 8, 11, 24, 32, 40
    Smiling Sam   32, 37, 39–40
animals of Australia   89
apostrophe   184
Australia   88–89, 90–92, 98–101, 106–108, 113–116, 155
boxing   145–146
building materials   190–191, 213
Canada   73–74, 126–130, 135–138, 146–149, 152–154, 275
cargo ship   113–116, 120–123, 127–128
cave people   259, 261–262
championship game   30–33, 37–41
circus   129–130, 133–138, 146
circus acts   133–134, 129–130, 135–138, 146
circus tent   133
city of the future   267–270
coach Denny   2, 23–24, 39–40
Columbus   277, 297
Concord   308–309, 314–318
contractions   184–187
dog   278–279, 289–292, 297–300, 324, 328
earthquake   215
Egypt   221–222, 224–225, 229–232, 239–241, 244–246
England   313–315
English soldiers   318, 324–325
Eric and Tom
    cave people   258, 261–262
    city of the future   267–270

Eric and Tom continued
>   Concord   308–309, 314–318
>   dogs   278–279, 289–292, 297–300, 324, 328
>   earthquake   215
>   Egypt   221–222, 224–225, 229–232, 239–241, 244–246
>   force   191, 203, 223, 246, 254, 259, 267, 270, 292, 308, 326
>   Greece   51, 251–254
>   horses   259–260
>   king of Egypt   241, 244–245
>   lion   246, 252
>   mammoth   259, 261
>   mummies   222
>   palace   231, 239–241
>   pyramids   222, 224–225, 245
>   Robert   316–318, 324–325
>   saber-toothed tiger   259–260
>   San Francisco   211–215
>   Spain   275, 276–279
>   sun god   231–232, 239–241
>   Thrig   201–202, 326
>   time machine   200–203, 211, 220, 223–225, 246, 254,
>   259–262, 267–270, 278–279, 289–292, 307–309, 324–326
>   Tom is lost   308–309, 314
>   Troy   251, 254
>   Vikings   292, 296–300, 306–308

force   191, 203, 223, 246, 254, 259, 267, 270, 292, 308, 326

future time   191–194, 201–202, 210–211, 220, 228–229,
    266–270, 274–275, 288–289, 304–305, 322–323

Greece   51, 251–254

Helen   251

Hohoboho
>   back-row words   64–66
>   contractions   185–187
>   fighting stops   173–175
>   Friday announcements   74–77, 81–84
>   homonyms   160–162, 167–168, 173–175

Hohoboho continued
    rules for seating   58–59
    words with the same spelling   178–181
    words with scars   161–162, 167–168
homonyms   160–162, 167–168, 173–175
horses   259–260
inventing   238–239
Italy 47, 50–51, 275
Japan   47
kangaroos   97–98
    Toby, the kangaroo   90–92, 98–101, 106–108, 113–116,
        120–123, 127–130, 135–138, 146–149, 152–155
    lookouts   99, 101, 114–115
king of Egypt   241, 244–245
koala   89
lion   246, 252
lookouts   99, 101
Mabel   100–101, 106–108, 113–114, 120–123, 128–129,
    146–148, 154–155
mammoth   259, 261
Mean George 4–5, 8, 11, 24, 32, 40
Mexico   275
minutes   112
mummies   222
Nile River   221, 245
North America   275
ocean liners   49
Pacific Ocean   46, 88–89
palace   231, 239–241
parts of a ship   113
past time   191–194, 201, 210–211, 220, 228–229, 266–267,
    274–275, 288–289, 304–305, 322–323
peacock   105, 115–116, 120–123, 127, 129–130, 148, 154–155
Pip   115–116, 120–123, 127, 129–130, 148, 154–155
platypus   89, 154–155
present-day travel   52

pyramids   222, 224–225, 245
Robert   316–318, 324–325
rule about time   192
saber–toothed tiger   259–260
San Francisco   211–215
seconds   112
sailing ships   48–50, 276, 292
Smiling Sam   32, 37, 39–40
Spain   275, 276–279
sun god   231–232, 239–241
Thrig   201–202, 326
time   112
time lines   193–194, 201, 210–211, 220, 228–229, 266–267, 274–275, 288–289, 304–305, 322–323
time machines   191, 200–203, 211, 220–223, 246, 254, 259–262, 267–270, 278–279, 289–292, 307–309, 324–326
Toby
    in Australia   90–92, 98–101, 106–108, 113–116
    in a circus   129–130, 135–138, 146
    in a zoo   148–149, 152–154
    in Canada   127–130, 135–138, 146–149, 152–154
    Mabel   100–101, 106–108, 113–114, 120–123, 128–129, 146–148, 154–155
    meets his father   148
    meets Pip   115
    on the ship   114–116, 120–123, 127–128
    returns to Australia   155
Tom, see **Eric and Tom**
treasures
    looking for sunken treasures   50–52
    ocean liners   49
    present-day travel   52
    sailing ships   48–50, 276, 292
Troy   251, 254
Turkey   47, 50–51
United States   46, 126–127, 275, 313–315, 318

words with scars

Vikings   292, 296–300, 306–308
Washington, George   314, 318, 324
wooden buildings   190–191, 213
words with the same spelling   178–181
words with scars   161–162, 167–168